RPA in Oracle

Anand Rajendran
Anil Appanaboyina
Gopikrishna Kakuru
Nagaraju Mutakaratapu

DOYENSYS
Technology Drives, We Lead

notionpress
.com

INDIA · SINGAPORE · MALAYSIA

Notion Press

Old No. 38, New No. 6
McNichols Road, Chetpet
Chennai - 600 031

First Published by Notion Press 2019
Copyright © Doyensys 2019
All Rights Reserved.

ISBN 978-1-64760-812-5

TABLE OF CONTENTS

CONTENTS

AUTOMATION

OBJECTIVE

The objective of this chapter (Automation) is to provide information on how Automation evolved and what are the different types of Automation currently available.

INTRODUCTION – AUTOMATION

Automation or Computerization is the innovation by which a procedure or system is performed with insignificant human help. Robotization or programmed control is the utilization of different equipment for working, for example, apparatus, forms in production lines, boilers and warmth treating broilers, turning on phone systems, directing and adjustment of boats, airship and different applications and vehicles with insignificant or diminished human intercession.

Automation covers applications running from an indoor family regulator controlling a kettle, to an enormous mechanical control framework with ten of thousands of information estimations and yield control signals. In control unpredictability, it can go from basic on-off control to multi-variable elevated level calculations.

Automation is the formation of innovation and its application to control and screen the creation and conveyance of different products and enterprises. It performs tasks that were recently performed by people. Automation is being utilized in various regions, for example, fabricating, transport, utilities, barrier, offices, activities and of late, data innovation.

Automation can be performed from various perspectives in different enterprises. For instance, in the data innovation space, product content can test a product item and produce a report. There are likewise different programming instruments accessible in the market which can create code for an application. The clients need to arrange the apparatus and characterize the procedure. In different ventures, robotization is incredibly improving profitability, sparing time and cutting expenses.

Automation is advancing rapidly and business insight in applications is another type of great mechanization. In the innovation space, the effect of computerization is expanding quickly, both in the product/equipment and machine layer. Notwithstanding, in spite of advances in mechanization, some manual mediation is constantly prompted, regardless of whether the apparatus can perform the greater part of the tasks.

What is Automation?

Automation is the technology by which a method or procedure is performed with nominal human help. Automation is the use of various control systems for operating instrumentation like machinery in the shop floor, processes in industries, switching on telephone networks, steering and stabilization of ships, aircraft etc. With nominal or reduced human intervention.

Automation is the creation of technology and its application to manage and monitor the assembly and delivery of various products and services. Automation can be performed in many ways in various industries for instance, within the information technology (IT) domain, a software script will test a software application or process and produce a report.

The users solely got to assemble the tools and define the process.

Automation helps in greatly improving productivity, saving time and cutting costs.

In the technology domain, the impact of automation is increasing rapidly, both within the software and hardware and machine layer.

Automation, as the term suggests, is the automatic execution of actions without the periodic intervention of humans or limited intervention of humans. A software system that operates on its own and an electronic device that functions autonomously are examples of automation.

Automatic devices monitor steps on their own, leading to cost optimization and timeline management. This additionally facilitates the identification of issues and subsequent mitigation to confirm seamless performance. Possible applications of automation technologies are many and unlimited ranging from single tasks to additional complicated, interconnected algorithms, dependent upon the actions of users or environments.

In the coming years, nearly all IT groups and business leaders will entertain the concept of automating some facets of their businesses.

Desktop Automation

Desktop automation is a robotic method automation scaled down for one user. Desktop automation tools install on one machine for one user and help individuals solve the issues within their sphere.

Desktop automation tools have bots also known as a web robot, robot or simply bot, that interact with websites, log into applications, pull data from excel files, transfer files, generate reports, and far more.

Business users like client Service representatives will simplify their tasks with desktop application automation and automated call setup. And IT can automatize workflows using any of the tasks in the list to eliminate tedious, manual tasks and eliminate the error.

Such applications have following features

- Application runs in single memory (Front end and back end in one place)
- Single user only (operating system user account)
- generally, no resource sharing (files and databases)
- State of an application can be nearly always determined
- Access to the local filing system

We have many tools to implement automation, the purpose of every tool is different and the implementation engineer ought to remember that. There are tools that work better with applications containing custom controls, some tools are economical and good for small applications and there are even tools that are quite good for beginners in automation and coding knowledge is also not required.

We have explained below the details of the desktop automation tools that are being used extensively by various business organizations and the information about these tools are shared from their respective company websites

Oracle Application Testing Suite – Oracle Application Testing Suite (OATS) contains a bunch of integrated products to help with Oracle Functional Testing for regression testing of Web applications, and Oracle Load Testing for performance testing of your Oracle packaged solutions. Oracle explains that its Application Testing Suite is a comprehensive, integrated testing solution that ensures the quality, scalability, and availability of your Web applications, Web Services, packaged Oracle Applications, and Oracle databases.

SikuliX – SikuliX can help automate anything you see on the screen of your desktop computer running Windows, Mac or some Linux/Unix. SikuliX uses image recognition powered by OpenCV to identify and control GUI components.

FlaUI – FlaUI is a .NET library that helps with automated test scripts for Windows user interface applications (Win32, WinForms, WPF, Store Apps. FlaUI was developed because of one of the maintainers of TestStack.White found White's codebase to be horrible to update and support.

AutoIt – AutoIt v3 is a freeware, BASIC-like scripting language designed for automating the Windows GUI and general scripting. While it's not the most robust of automated testing tools, many teams integrate AutoIt with Selenium to work around non-browser windows that appear in an automated test workflow.

ZAPTEST – ZAPTEST is one of those tools I've heard about for a while but never tried until I heard that it now offers a free edition. ZAPTEST can be used to create test automation against any GUI-based application. It also supports any environment, making it a very flexible solution if you're looking for cross-operating system support.

Web Automation

Web automation replaces humans with an online software system for repetitive and tedious tasks, such as:

- Form filling
- Screen scraping
- Data extraction and transfer between applications
- Website testing
- Periodical report generation

Small businesses, large enterprises have the benefit of web-based automation solutions.

Most part of web automation is browser automation. It aims to mimic how user's use web browsers to automate repetitive tasks or scenarios. As it usually happens with a computer trying to be a human, the process gets complex and fragile. This complexity is an effect of following inherent properties of the task:

- Browser interactions are based on HTML markup, which is rarely composed with this thought in mind.
- HTML structure is rigid and changes often.
- Browsers communicate through network inheriting all its failures and unreliability.

But sometimes it's the only option to extract content from the remote system. Many paid solutions, as well as free libraries, attempt to simplify web scraping.

Web Testing: The majority of software now comes in the form of Web-based applications that are run in an Internet browser such as Chrome, Internet Explorer, or Firefox. Many users assume of a browser as just a way of displaying information, but anyone who develops applications knows how capable and important they are—and how crucial a cross-browser testing tool for testing any application intended to run on them is.

Web browser automation supports testing in two ways:

- In quality assurance (QA) testing in the development process. These tests are run while developing the application to ensure basic functionality.

- In testing performance during implementation, to help support the high level of service demanded by customers. These tests need to be run frequently, particularly when there is any change to the configuration.

Automation makes planning more important and effective. You have to be clear on what test cases are most crucial, and you need to test them with the right, high-quality data, which can take some effort to generate. This is called establishing a test automation framework, a set of useful guidelines for managing your testing and ensuring the most beneficial results. And, of course, there is still a large place for manual website testing.

But an automation tool does make it easier for you to test early in the process, test frequently, and continue testing after the product is operational. Early testing in QA identifies problems before they get baked into the design, and in implementation identifies problems that provide a poor user experience.

The point of automated website testing is to help you accentuate the negative. It's easy to think of tests that can provide a lot of data, but are not likely to find defects. That makes you look busy and productive, but often fails to uncover real problems.

Always be adding other scenarios, other possible actions, other mistakes users might make. A lot of users means a lot of creative mistakes you had not considered. Have you thought through every possible test case? Automation helps you manage and anticipate these mistakes.

Web Data Extraction: Going out to get data is the flip side of automating the testing of your website or web application. It is you going out and acquiring data from other websites and bringing it back to enable your own functions. This can be called a variety of things, including web scraping, web harvesting, and web data extraction. Websites have a lot of data, but it not usually easy to download, and requires the use of the browser.

Business uses include pricing intelligence, to know what the pricing on other sites is. If you provide a catalog, getting the information to populate it is not a trivial matter. Companies also monitor their brand, sentiment, and mentions to track what people are saying, and thus the value of their brand and their reputation. A scripting interface can save data directly to your own databases.

Back-office Automation

Back-office automation efforts are considered to reduce manual processes and provide an essential framework for getting work done accurately and faster.

Some back-office areas that can leverage automation software include:

- Finance
- Human Resources
- IT
- Marketing
- Sales
- Compliance
- Product Development
- Security/Maintenance

In many cases, even for large organizations, software applications and processes routinely amount to people sending an email with spreadsheets and documents around for review. These are not the best ways to handle the flow of information in an organization between people and systems. All these manual methods are more likely to frustrate and impede business goals rather than accomplish them.

Manual systems ensure:

- Information is lost
- Stakeholders experience frequent interruptions
- Mistakes and misunderstandings occur regularly
- Deadlines are missed
- Communication is difficult
- Data is re-entered multiple times
- Reporting and monitoring the process is impossible
- There is no audit trail

Systems designed to automate back-office processes can handle all of these issues and much more. Information stays within the system at all times. Requests, approvals and all other related documents and communication are forever retained within the system.

Stakeholders are only alerted when there is an action for them to take (no more "Reply All" emails) and taking action like approving a request requires a few clicks.

Mistakes and misunderstandings are greatly reduced because there is only one information source of record. Activities and communications are all visible. Deadlines are much more likely to be met thanks to alerts, reminders, and infinitely less time spent searching for people and information. Communication is streamlined and tied closely to the process itself. So that alert only those who need to see it.

Data is entered numerous times, instead enter information once, pass it through the process and then push it into another application if needed. Transaction reporting and monitoring tools are built into the system and allow complete visibility into performance and monitor all activity through dashboards. Audit trails are also built into the system, allowing a permanent, shareable record of all transactions and activities.

Back-office automation has lots of benefits like reducing stress in carrying out daily work, saving time spent on repetitive tasks, improve the productivity of the individual and also boosting individual creativity, better customer service, and cost-efficient. The process of maintaining physical documents is tedious and unreliable but automation and technology which support cloud-based storage will make it easier to access the documents from anywhere and during an audit.

In the back office, automation supports in a lot of areas, such as maintaining inventory, keeping paperwork in an organized manner, streamlined communication between team members and electronic data storage for easy access to records.

Business Process Automation

A general innovation term that is utilized to depict any procedure being robotized using PCs and PC programming. Procedures that have been mechanized require less human intercession and less human time to convey.

Business Process Automation (BPA), otherwise called business robotization or digital transformation, is the innovation empowered mechanization of complex business forms. It can streamline business for straightforwardness, accomplish computerized change, increment administration quality, improve administration conveyance or contain costs. It comprises of incorporating applications, rebuilding work assets and utilizing programming applications all through the association. Mechanical procedure robotization is a developing field inside BPA and utilizations human-made consciousness.

BPA is a method for mechanizing repeating business forms using programming and distinctive application reconciliations. This means, rather than having your representatives to humble and basic undertakings, you let the product deal with it.

Business Process Automation can either totally remain solitary (robotizing a few organization forms) or be a piece of a bigger activity, for example,

- **Business Process Improvement (BPI)** – discovering dull procedures and improving them. In BPI, computerization can either be a major piece of it (in general improvement through mechanization), or only a small confound piece (robotizing a stage in a procedure).
- **Business Process Re-Engineering (BPR)** – BPR works pretty much equivalent to BPI, with the principle distinction being that it focuses or centers on tearing down and reconstructing forms from scratch. Robotization will in general have a major impact on BPR activities; by and large, in case you're re-structuring a procedure, this is a result of new advancements.
- **Business Process Management (BPM)** – BPM is a technique of nonstop improvement – in contrast to BPI or BPR, the two of which are one-time activities, BPM is something an organization does deliberately. As needs are, BPA can influence in streamlining and mechanizing old procedures.

BPA Principles

Three main principle fundamentals in BPA:

- It enables organizations to coordinate, incorporate, and consequently execute.
- It brings together your procedures for the best measure of straightforwardness, as it keeps the processing engineering flawless. It combines the business capacities that ought to coherently be progressively incorporated and spreads them out over the organization.
- It tends to your human-driven assignments and limits the requirement for individual collaboration.

Automation Types

There are four sorts of Automation (robotization), advancing in intricacy:

- **Essential Automation:** Basic robotization focuses are the basic occupations in your association, giving a brought together spot to store all related data. For instance, utilizing a unified informing apparatus for a theme or gathering permits straightforwardness in correspondence, rather than concealing data in different email accounts.

- **Procedure Automation:** This archives and deals with your business forms for assignment consistency and straightforwardness. It is more dominant than fundamental mechanization and can be constrained by devoted programming and applications.

- **Reconciliation Automation:** More mind-boggling than procedure robotization, coordination mechanization empowers machines to watch how people perform errands and rehash those activities. People must characterize the standards, notwithstanding. For instance, you could coordinate your BPM programming and client care programming. This could give you results from a client care agenda handled for every client grumbling and allot workforce when required.

- **Computerized reasoning or Artificial Intelligence (AI) Automation:** Adding AI to incorporation programming empowers basic leadership where your innovative help is humanlike. The framework would settle on choices on how to manage the information, given what it has realized and always dissected. For instance, in assembling, AI Automation can altogether decrease supply chain forecasting errors or blunders.

The Elements of Business Process Automation

Most BPA endeavors or efforts include three components:

- Business standards and rationale or logic
- Organized information
- Unstructured information

Business standards and rationale incorporate the stipulations, reasons, information, and records that help your business parameters. A portion of this rationale might be completely computerized, while different parts should be checked on by somebody associated with the procedure.

Organized information is the data in your endeavor applications that you reference when making procedure refreshes. This information is profoundly sorted out and effectively recognizable via web search tool calculations, as it shows up in fixed fields inside your records or documents. Machines can create organized information, (for example, fabricating sensors that produce the temperature of revolution check), thus can people, (for example, those rounding out the age, sex, or ZIP code fields of a structure).

While unstructured information is progressively emotional and as a rule very message substantial, it is critical, as most data used to settle on business choices is unstructured. This information can emerge out of numerous sources (for instance, web-based life) and is hard to place into an organized organization of sections and columns for simple extraction and investigation. BPA stages expect to flawlessly coordinate these three components.

The BPA programming frameworks that you can discover or support to help your automation may vary by whether they can address AI and progressed or advanced analytics.

BPA can address these parts of process design

The capacity to survey process work processes and overhaul or redesign

Help in figuring out what automation components are required and how they fit into the bigger business situation

The capacity to convey quickened verifications of idea utilizing indicated arrangements

Integration of AI

BPA Phases

The periods of BPA:

- **Investigation:** In this stage, you audit your association's framework. Survey its prerequisites and targets before playing out a full audit of the present frameworks, information needs, and business forms. At that point select an innovation arrangement dependent on its engineering structure and its fit with the business. At this stage, outside advisors who are specialists in the innovation are useful.

- **Usage:** During this stage, set up and modify the innovation. On the off chance that vital, expand the present IT frameworks with particular modules and additional items. As of now, documentation is basic, and you should record every single usefulness. You ought to likewise actualize chairman and select end-client preparing, trailed by start to finish and client acknowledgment testing to decide attainability before the following stage.

- **Incorporation:** At this stage, perform API reconciliation. This empowers the new projects to get to and speak with other existing projects. You ought to likewise perform information coordination during this progression, consolidating information from divergent sources. Finally, execute the venture administration transport (ESB) in an administration arranged engineering (SOA). An ESB permits correspondence between programming applications.

- **Upkeep and Support:** This last eliminate looks for bottlenecks and blemishes in your procedures with the goal that they can be adjusted. You ought to constantly refresh your framework renditions, with predictable movement to new stages as they are accessible. The entire association ought to likewise have the option to exploit specialized help.

CONCLUSION

From the topics discussed above, it is understandable that there are wide possibilities for Automation. Whatever process the client is following, there is a scope of automation in it. This helps in saving time and that can be effectively used for another important task for the organization.

BASICS OF RPA

OBJECTIVE

The objective of this chapter - Basics of Robotic Process Automation is to provide information on how RPA evolved and Tools currently available.

INTRODUCTION – RPA BASICS

Consider RPA a blend of Artificial Intelligence (AI) and Software programming Automation. Basically, it enables organizations to arrange PC programming to gather and concentrate information, perceive designs, and learn, adjust and react to new circumstances.

RPA is not the same as a standard PC program, one that acts in a static, typically direct design. RPA is dynamic – it searches for examples and makes expectations. RPA can be arranged to "watch" the manner in which a prepared client plays out a specific errand and the different choice focuses associated with achieving that undertaking, and with recreating the procedure.

What is Robotic Process Automation?

RPA alludes to the utilization of programming "robots" that mimic tasks performed by people. These robots are particularly useful for computerizing rule-based procedures that require association with various, unique IT systems.

Mechanical Process Automation is an insightful method for taking a shot at errands that can without much of a stretch be ordered by the utilization of Artificial Intelligence (AI). It very well may be separated as

Automated: Machines that copy human activities are called Robots.

Procedure: Sequence of steps that lead to a significant movement. For instance:- the way toward making tea or the way toward making your preferred dish and so forth.

Automation: Any procedure which is finished by a robot without human mediation.

To summarize, imitating human activities to play out an arrangement of steps that lead to a significant movement, with no human mediation is known as Robotic Process Automation.

It is broadly anticipated that in the Fourth Industrial Revolution, administrative work will be robotized the manner in which mechanical apply mechanized autonomy creation on the shop floor.

RPA can be utilized to computerize work processes, framework, back-office process which are work concentrated. These product bots can connect with an in-house application, site, client entrance, and so forth. The RPA is a product program that keeps running on an end client's pc, workstation or cell phone. It is a grouping of directions which are executed by Bots under some characterized set of business rules.

The fundamental objective of Robotics process is the robotization procedure to supplant dull and exhausting administrative assignment performed by people with a virtual workforce. RPA doesn't require the advancement of code, nor does it require direct access to the code or database of the applications.

Automation existed even before RPA came into the image. Despite the fact that various covers exist between these two, not at all like RPA, Automation is the creation of another innovation to take care of genuine issues with the requirement for human mediation.

S.No	Feature	Automation	RPA
1	What does it Reduce?	Reduces execution time	Reduces the number of people working on something.
2	What does it automate?	Automates repetitive test cases i.e a product	Automates the repetitive business process i.e product as well as business
3	Programming Knowledge	Programming knowledge required to create test scripts	Programming knowledge is mostly not needed as it is wizard-driven
4	Software Environment	Limited software environment	A wide range of software environments
5	Application	Used for QA, Production, Performance, UAT environments	Usually used in production environments

Example – Consider an occasion, where you need to distribute your articles on different social gatherings at a particular time each day. OK wish to do it physically yourself or would you choose a representative whose sole occupation is distributing articles regularly?

This would cost you a great deal, and furthermore it would be tedious for that worker. Is it safe to say that it isn't?

Rather, you could simply cause a robot to do it for you! You could simply design a PC programming or a robot to translate the human activities and copy them. In this way, here you could simply arrange a robot to distribute the articles each day at the referenced time. That would cost you less as well as be less tedious. Along these lines, emulating human activities to play out a grouping of steps that lead to an important movement, with no human intercession is known as Robotic Process Automation.

RPA History

There are 3 basic abilities that make up a cutting edge RPA organization:

Screen scraping, Business Process Automation and Artificial Intelligence.

As Robert Rennie clarifies the antecedents of RPA were basic screen scraping projects worked for testing Automation. Both driving (UiPath) and rising (Argos Labs) RPA organizations have their underlying foundations in screen scraping. For Automation of testing or different assignments, organizations need successful screen scraping arrangements.

After some time, financials related establishments working with these screen scraping were able to robotize complex procedures. This permitted developing RPA organizations to construct business process robotization solutions over their screen scrapers. Business process Automation (BPA) solutions existed since the 1990s and they were at that point very experienced so there was not unreasonably much research expected to tie BPA to screen scrapers.

With the ascent of AI, organizations turned out to be progressively mindful that machines could outperform people in basic psychological undertakings like OCR or example acknowledgment. The RPA designers that we realize today were conceived as they added AI capacities to their product with organizations and through their commercial centers.

Test Automation Vs RPA

A noteworthy distinction between Test Automation and RPA is that test automation lives with the context of test conditions and uses test information or data. (Often masked), while RPA clearly works in production environment using real-time business data.

Due to this reason, RPA tools always keep track of all changes made by users and track everything the RPA bots have done. Complete audit trails for each step is mandatory and vital

Most test automation devices are not suitable for RPA on the grounds that they do not maintain enterprise features of governance, audit trails and taking changes.

For long-term strategic reasons, when choosing an automation platform, it makes sense to pick one that isn't "just" made for test automation. Instead think of process automation more broadly, and research tools that can be used across the enterprise.

To summarize, test automation is the process of automating the testing process i.e. building code or software to perform the task of manual testing.

These different types of tools are available in the market, both open source and paid.

The key goal is to build a product with great quality by spending less time in testing.

Robotic Process Automation – It is the process of automating the business process in industries like Telecom, Pharma, Banking, etc.. using the software robots to accomplish the tasks

For these different types of RPA tools are available in the market, like UiPath, Automation Anywhere, Blue prism, etc.

The key goal is to automate the business process to cut down manual labor cost and time, without compromising the accuracy

Testing Tools

- Traditional automation tool is designed specifically for testing only for GUI or Web-based systems.
- Test Automation is applied only to the product and its features.
- Test automation works across different environments, i.e., QA, UAT, Prod, etc
- Test Automation is limited to QA
- Developing all advance features will depend on the testing tool. And not sure even if it will support.
- In traditional automation we cannot automate any application until we do not have instance of that application (which needs to automate). E.g. web applications URL, or Windows application exe. path required for automation.

RPA Tools

- RPA tools can easily automate processes spanning across interfaces like legacy systems, virtual machines, both desktop and web-based applications, backend process etc.
- RPA could be applied to other business processes, with or without a user interface.
- RPA meant to runs only in the production environment.
- RPA systems could be used by all individuals across the firm in terms of creation and usage.
- Most of these tools have the ready to use features that speeds up process design (through ready process templates) and implementation into the RPA container.

☐ RPA tool can automate applications even if you don't have direct access to the application (URL/EXE).Assume you need to automate some applications which are installed on virtual machine and its URL/EXE cannot access from outside.

Attended Vs Unattended RPA

Robotic Process Automation enables organizations with tools to create their own software robots to automate any business process and these are called as digital workers or bots.

Digital Workers (or Bots) are configurable software set up to perform the tasks you assign and control and these bots are seen to be faster. More accurate, secure and compliant.

There can be attended bots or unattended bots. As you think about processes, it should be obvious that a number of them are handed off to a robot fully without any human intervention required and this is called unattended bots.

Some processes will still need the human touch they are called attended bots.

RPA bots will work in both "attended" and "unattended" modes. Usually targeted toward front-office activities, attended bots are helpful when the whole end-to-end process can't be machine-driven. Bots will work alongside humans to deliver attended automation. In such cases, the actions of RPA bots can still be triggered by system-level events that will provide and take information to and from human staff. Attended automation employs desktop robots to automatize repetitive desktop tasks. Desktop robots allow staff sitting at those desktop screens with correct info and steering once and wherever it's required, this way staff increase productivity and helps in efficiently service the customers.

Unattended RPA bots execute tasks and interact with applications independent of human involvement. Unattended bots are triggered by events and that they can be scheduled. Unattended bots usually perform batch operations that don't need user intervention. for instance, a batch of new customer information is received in a very computer program and desires to be entered into multiple applications. Attended bots optimize tasks by offloading parts of them, serving to work get done quicker. Unattended bots execute tasks and move with applications freelance of human involvement. The mixture of attended and unattended RPA provides for an entire RPA resolution.

Bots complete business processes without the human intervention per a preset schedule Frees staff from repetitive work and helps in completing the work faster and cost-effectively.

Current RPA solutions tend to profit human-involved processes with straightforward tasks and structured knowledge at a high volume. It's anticipated that RPA solutions can still evolve to having the ability to handle unstructured knowledge and sophisticated tasks.

RPA Vs AI

RPA is a software system robot that mimics human actions, whereas Artificial intelligence (AI) is the creation of intelligent machines that work and react like humans like Speech Recognition software.

RPA is related to "doing" whereas AI and Machine Learning (ML) are concerned with "thinking" and "learning" respectively.

For Example: Your suppliers send you the electronic invoices by email, you download the invoices into a folder, extract the relevant info from the supplier invoices, and eventually produce the bills in your ERP (Oracle) System. In this situation, RPA is appropriate for automating the grunt work of retrieving emails, downloading the attachments (i.e. invoices) into an outlined folder, and make the bills in the (ERP) accounting software system.

On the other hand, AI is required to intelligently "read" the supplier invoices, and extract the appropriate info like invoice number, supplier name, invoice due date, product description, amounts due etc., because the invoices are primarily unstructured or at the best, semi-structured information because different suppliers have different invoice templates and formats.

To be sure, it's possible to handle invoice processing through RPA alone. In this case, we'll deploy what's normally referred to as attended automation. Attended automation, or Robotic Desktop Automation (RDA), is sort of a virtual assistant that works hand-in-hand along with your human staff.

Going back to our example, after the invoices are downloaded, they'll be passed through an Optical Character Recognition (OCR) software system which can decide to extract the specified info and a human operator can then validate these info, before handing over the work back to the RPA bot to create the invoices within the system.

Another key distinction between RPA and AI lies in their focus.

RPA is extremely process-driven — it's all about automating repetitive, rule-based processes that usually need interaction with multiple, IT systems.

AI, on the other hand, is about data.

Thereafter, the task is to pick an appropriate ml formula, and then train the algorithm sufficiently so it's ready to acknowledge other new invoices quicker and more accurately than a human might.

At the end of the day, RPA and AI are valuable tools that you can use to assist your organization's digital transformation.

RPA Benefits

What will RPA do for your organization? You'll see vital and measurable enhancements in a very range of areas like

Customer satisfaction: By liberating up your customer-service personnel from forms and tabulations, you're creating all of them a lot of obtainable for attentive client service. You're additionally reducing the chance for errors. The result's a rise in client satisfaction and far larger ability to fulfill the necessities of service-level agreements.

Productivity: Compared with humans, digital workers can finish a task 5 times quicker. They additionally work 24/7 and don't require any holidays and there is an increase in productivity associated with those tasks, you've additionally freed workers for unstructured problem-solving. You're increasing their satisfaction and potency, which boosts productivity even more.

Accuracy: Humans create mistakes. Robots are 100% correct, 100% consistent, and 100% compliant with policies. The additional you switch over to robots, the less clerical errors show your expertise, and also the longer you save that accustomed be spent correcting those errors.

Resource utilization: Offloading the mundane or boring tasks to robots frees up your team to handle the tasks that add the foremost worth to your business. Employees can now be involved in more productive and result in orient tasks. That's sensible for client service and helps ease time unit headaches.

Return on investment (ROI): All types of enhancements will yield positive ROI, together with each technological advancements and upgrades in your human men. What's notable concerning your robotic men, when you flip the switch, is that your ROI shows up with lightning speed. Your in-operation prices can drop quickly, and everybody likes ROI that doesn't take forever to point out au courant rock bottom line.

Compliance benefits: Due to RPA, human contact with sensitive information may be decreased, reducing chance of fraud and compliance problems. The audit path is maintained, permitting elaborate audit just in case problems arise.

RPA Risks

Risk is the possibility of losing something of value. With RPA characterized by no or very little intervention by human beings, risk management plays a pivotal role in RPA implementation. Here are some key risks and controls you should consider while implementing RPA or planning our RPA journey:

- A lack of standardization of processes – this often leads to solutions being customized to countries and business units, resulting in errors and increased cost of automation. Prior to RPA implementation, organizations should first standardize the major part of their process the processes across geographies and business units.
- A lack of ownership, roles and responsibilities – functional heads tend to think that a particular technology solution is owned by IT, while IT think of themselves as just the enabler and the functional heads as solution owners. This leads to a situation where nobody owns the errors and problems of automation. Organizations should clearly define the ownership, roles, and responsibilities of each of the stakeholders within any RPA solutions they adopt.

- Data privacy and cybersecurity – RPA implementation comes with a number of risks and internal privileged access rights that have the potential to be exploited. This can lead to the confidentiality, integrity, and reliability of data that the organization processes being compromised. Organizations should deploy adequate cybersecurity and data privacy controls, depending on the data exposure and extent of personal data available within the organization.

- A lack of effective change management process – as the level of automation within an organization develops, data mapping and configuration will also change. If the related configurations and data-mapping aren't updated within the automated solution, it will deliver inaccurate results and the incorrect output. Organizations should define and adopt a strong change management process to mitigate this risk.

- Data flow – In order to implement RPA securely, firms need to make sure the data flow is understood. Day-to-day users of desktop automation need to be trained on data policies and fully refreshed every six months. At the same time, data should be encrypted. And of course, identity and access management are important

- Development processes – Many of the security risks in RPA emerge due to issues within the development process. Securing RPA calls for a holistic approach including governance

- Process documentation – in many cases, process documentation is not updated, making it difficult to manage changes at a later date in the application. Organizations should ensure that all documents, supplier information, inputs, RPA logic processing, outputs, customer information are updated, which enables any changes to be easily implemented, when required.

- Selection of the automation tool and partner – failure to invest in the right tools and partner can directly impact the viability and outcome of an organization's automation journey. Inappropriate investment can lead to a waste of time and money. Organizations should perform adequate due diligence while selecting an RPA partner and an automation tool.

RPA Tools

Given below is a list of popular RPA Tools.

Blue Prism

Blue Prism RPA provides all core features. It can work on any platform with any application. For using this tool you should have programming skills but it is user-friendly for developers. This tool is perfect for medium and large organizations.

Features:

- It supports the multi-environment preparation model.
- Security provided for network and software system credentials.
- It is used on any platform.
- Work for any application.

Advantages:

- High-speed execution.
- Platform independence.

Inflectra Rapise

Rapise is the next generation software test automation tool that leverages the power of open and extensible architecture to provide the most rapid, flexible functional testing application in the market as on date. We can record or create a test script and execute the same script without modification across the browsers and platforms. Rapise provides support for hybrid business situations. Rapise is on-premise solution.

This tool is ideal for small and medium organizations

Features

- Supports automation projects of any size
- Record and play functionality
- Internet & desktop automation; internet and screen scraping

- REST and SOAP calls and email processing (Gmail, Office 365, personal mail servers). SOAP (Simple Object Access Protocol) and REST (Representational State Transfer) are both web service communication protocols.
- Provides an open platform for enhancements and integration
- Provides special support for Microsoft Dynamics applications

Advantages

- Non-developer friendly
- Rapise supports with coaching and certifications.
- Quick and easy execution.

UiPath

UiPath provides all core capabilities. It provides support for Citrix and easy for non-developers too. It will handle advanced processes and this tool is ideal for any size of business.

Features:

- It provides security by managing credentials, providing encryption and access controls.
- It will automate quicker. 8 to 10 times quicker automation through Citrix too.
- Provides an open platform
- It will handle any method, in any range, or even complex scenarios

Advantages

- No programming skills needed.
- Easy use through drag and drop facility.

Automation Anywhere

Automation Anywhere provides all core capabilities. This tool can be used to automate both on-premise and cloud services. This user-friendly tool is ideal for medium and large organizations.

Features:

- Provides Bank-grade security
- Provides security through authentication, encryption, and credentials
- Real-time reports and analytics
- Provides platform independence

Advantages

- User-friendliness

Pega

Pega is a Business process Management tool. It is used on desktop servers. It provides solely cloud-based solutions or services. It will work on Windows, Linux, and Mac. This tool is ideal for medium and large business organizations.

Features:

- it'll assist you in the deployment of your solutions to the customers.
- It provides a cloud-based solution.
- It doesn't store any execution data in an exceeding database, rather everything gets stored in the memory.
- With this tool, you can distribute the work to desktop, server, and staff as well.

Advantages

- This tool is mostly used for the event-driven approach, hence it works faster.
- Very sturdy and reliable tool.

Contextor

This tool is ideal for any size front office. It provides on-premise and cloud services. It provides support for Citrix. It works for all digital computer applications.

Features:

- Contextor can communicate with the active applications additionally and also with the applications that are minimized.

- It will communicate with all digital computer applications in parallel.
- This tool supports Citrix and RDP hybrid virtualization environment.
- Contextor provides reports and analytics.

Advantages

- It is easily integrated with AI.

Nice Systems

Nice RPA tool is named as NEVA-Nice Employee Virtual Attendant. This tool helps the staff in repetitive tasks.

Features:

- It provides attended and unattended server automation.
- It will help you in automating mundane tasks like Compliance adherence and Up-sell.
- This system is made for employees from the back offices, Finance, HR etc.
- It provides cloud-based and on-premise solutions.

Advantages

- Provides advanced analytics

Kofax

Kofax can work with any application virtually. Coding skills are not mandatory for this tool. It can process data from any application or platform.

Features:

- It does repetitive tasks efficiently
- Intelligent tool for monitoring and optimizing the processes
- It can be managed centrally from a server
- Easy to integrate with Kapow Katalyst Platform

Advantages

- Efficient tool
- It can work fast

Kryon

Kryon RPA tool is named as Automate. It has three RPA solutions for automation. Unattended, Attended, and Hybrid. An unattended solution is an intelligent tool and can make decisions. Attended RPA tool will give you speed, accuracy, and efficiency at work. A hybrid automation tool is the combination of both attended and unattended automation.

Features:

- Kryon has attended, unattended and hybrid automation tools
- It is a scalable system
- It helps in improving efficiency
- This tool provides recording facility

Advantages

- Efficiently performs repetitive and time-consuming tasks
- It is user-friendly

Softomotive

Softomotive has two solutions for RPA. They are Enterprise Automation and Desktop Automation. Enterprise automation will help in increasing the performance, efficiency and productivity, of enterprises. Desktop automation is for individuals and small teams or organizations. Softomotive can automate desktop and web-based tasks.

Features:

- This tool will help you from the design process to the production process.
- It provides accuracy, security and error handling.
- It can be integrated with Oracle EBS, SAP, Salesforce, and PeopleSoft Automation etc.
- It is supported by SQL Server and .NET

Advantages

- Easy to use.
- It works five times faster than humans.

Visual Cron is a Windows-only automation tool for task scheduling and integration. Programming skills are not compulsory for this tool.

Features:

- You can customize tasks according to technology.
- You can do programming using the Application Programming Interface (API).
- User-friendly interface.
- No programming skills needed

Advantages

- Easy to learn.

CONCLUSION

From the topics discussed above, it is understandable that there are wide possibilities for Robotic Process Automation. Whatever process the client is following, there is a scope of RPA in it. This helps in saving time, manpower and that can be effectively used for another important task for the organization.

WORKFLOW AUTOMATION

OBJECTIVE

The objective of this chapter (Automation) is to provide information on how Automation evolved and what are the different types of Automation currently available.

INTRODUCTION – WORKFLOW AUTOMATION

Workflow Automation refers to the planning, execution, and automation of processes based on workflow rules wherever human tasks, data or files are routed between people or systems based on pre-defined business rules.

Workflow Basics

A work process is a succession of tasks that procedures a lot of data. Workflows happen over each sort of business and industry. Whenever information is passed among people or potentially frameworks, a work process is made. Work processes are the ways that portray how something goes from being fixed to done, or crude to prepare.

Essentially, a "workflow" is the means by which you complete work. It's a progression of tasks you have to finish in order to reach some repeatable business goals.

The keyword here is repeatable. The workflow process shouldn't be mistaken for an assignment (a one-an opportunity to-do), or a lot of tasks built together (that is an undertaking). It's a chain of tasks that occur in a grouping and something that you do all the time.

To give you a superior thought of how this functions, how about we spread a reasonable model: representative onboarding. At whatever point you enlist another representative, you have to clarify how the organization functions, what their job is, etc.

The sequence of tasks for a fruitful onboarding workflow process could be...

- ➢ Stage 1 – Send the new worker an invite letter
- ➢ Stage 2 – Get the representative to fill in statutory structures
- ➢ Stage 3 – Enter the representative's close to home data in the organization database
- ➢ Stage 4 – Get the contract's workstation prepared
- ➢ Stage 5 – Schedule any required preparing and workshops

Development: The possibility of work process started in the assembling area to facilitate tasks between individuals, current organizations have received the term to appreciate the accompanying key advantages:

- ➢ Improved proficiency
- ➢ Better responsiveness
- ➢ Work process straightforwardness
- ➢ Expanded productivity

Associations use work processes to facilitate assignments among individuals and synchronize information between frameworks, with a definitive objective of improving authoritative productivity, responsiveness and gainfulness.

Kinds of Workflow

There are three key kinds of work processes:

- ➢ Direct Workflow – ordinarily advances from one stage to straight away and doesn't step back.
- ➢ State Machine Workflow – ordinarily progress with reference to 'State' and return can to a past point whenever required.
- ➢ Standards Driven Workflow – handled by predefined decides that can empower required information catch, programmed task reassignment or different activities.

Human-Centric versus Framework Centric Workflows

In human-driven work processes, the vast majority of the undertakings are appointed to people. These might require endorsing information, making something new, or twofold checking data.

In framework driven work processes, the vast majority of the undertakings are finished by a machine and expect next to zero human association. For instance, to make a money related report, a work process may be activated simultaneously consistently to get certain information from various frameworks, parse it into a report, and email the report to every one of the partners. A framework can play out these undertakings.

There are additionally record driven work processes where the whole work process is worked around an archive. A genuine model is an agreement for renting some office space.

Everything that occurs as a piece of the work process should be included or altered the archive and the final product ought to be an agreement that accurately catches every one of the information in the work process including advanced marks.

Robotized versus Manual Workflows

In a manual work process, a human is in charge of pushing everything starting with one assignment then onto the next. For instance, when a representative rounds out a repayment guarantee, she should email it to her chief for endorsement. After endorsement, she should email it to the fund division.

The money division must go into the product and timetable an installment and after that email the representative to state it is finished.

In a robotized work process, when a human finishes an assignment, she isn't in charge of passing the information on to the following errand. The work process is customized to deal with this. The framework deals with the progression of tasks including notices, cutoff times, and updates.

In a similar repayment model, the worker may round out a structure and hit a submit catch. It would consequently trigger a notice for the director to survey it and snap Approve.

This would naturally take it to the money group for handling, or if the sum is little enough, it will trigger an errand to discharge the installments and send a computerized email to the worker.

Workflow Branching

Business procedure streams give a manual for individuals to complete work. They give a streamlined client experience that leads individuals through the procedures their association has characterized for cooperations that should be progressed to a finish or something to that affect. This client experience can be custom fitted so individuals with various security jobs can have an encounter that best suits the work they do.

Use business procedure streams to characterize a lot of steps for individuals to pursue to take them to an ideal result. These means give a visual marker that tells individuals where they are in the business procedure. Business procedure streams decrease the requirement for preparing in light of the fact that new clients don't need to concentrate on which substance they ought to utilize. They can give the procedure a chance to manage them. You can arrange business procedure streams to help basic deals systems that can help your business gatherings accomplish better outcomes. For administration gatherings, business procedure streams can enable new staff to get up-to-speed all the more rapidly and keep away from missteps that could bring about unsatisfied clients.

Business procedure streams manage you through different phases of offers, showcasing, or administration forms toward fruition. In basic cases, a direct business procedure stream is a decent choice. Be that as it may, in increasingly complex situations, you can improve a business procedure stream with stretching. On the off chance that you have the make authorizations on business procedure streams, you'll be capable make business procedure stream with numerous branches by utilizing the If-Else rationale. The spreading condition can be shaped by different coherent articulations that utilization a blend of AND OR.

Pay heed to the accompanying data when you structure the business procedure stream with the branches:

A procedure can length crosswise over one of a kind elements. You can utilize stages per procedure and steps per arrange. Expanding guidelines must be founded on the means in the phase that quickly goes before it.

You can consolidate numerous conditions in a standard by utilizing the AND administrator or the OR administrator, however not the two administrators.

When you characterize a procedure stream, you can alternatively choose an element relationship. This relationship should a 1:N (One-to-Many) substance relationship.

Beyond what one dynamic procedure can run simultaneously on a similar information record.

When combining branches, all companion branches must converge to a solitary stage. The friend branches should all either converge to a solitary stage, or each companion branch must end the procedure. A friend branch can't converge with different branches and simultaneously end the procedure.

There are two essential sorts of expanding you can use in your work process:

Fork Branch – the work process takes one way, or it takes another (for instance, either a P.O. is affirmed, or it isn't)

Parallel Branch – the work process has assignments that can be finished at the same time by various clients (instead of successively)

Workflow Development

Making a work process for a procedure, includes characterizing forms that should be overseen all through the association, which may incorporate repeatable undertakings and gathered assignments. It likewise requires imagining, estimating, controlling, revealing, and, improving that procedure after some time, to build profitability as well as lessening costs.

Flowcharts and different outlines can be utilized for venture arranging, framework mapping, process documentation, or making practically any sort of work process. Be that as it may, not all flowcharts are made equivalent as far as helping you accomplish your definitive result.

There are a couple of various flowchart types, including your essential flowchart for undertaking arranging just as those progressively appropriate for sorting out complex procedures, similar to the swimlane outline.

They can be valuable when sorting out a procedure that includes a progression of assignments, such as handling a client's structure. You can even make a work process to follow your different work processes.

Building Your Workflow Flowchart

Here is a general thought of what the association procedure ought to resemble all the way:

Stage 1: Name your work process. The name should enable you to distinguish your definitive result, however don't stress a lot over this, as you can transform it later.

Stage 2: Identify the start and end focus. What occasions or undertakings will trigger the procedure to begin? By what means will you know when your result has been come to?

Stage 3: Identify what is expected to play out the procedure. What assignments, records, and genuine materials (paper, pens, mechanization programming, programs, and so forth.) are expected to finish the procedure?

Stage 4: List any tasks and exercises. What should be done to achieve your result? Express these in an action word/object group (for example affirm the solicitation, sign the desk work, and so forth.). Each errand may get its own container in your flowchart or chart, so you can assemble minor assignments if fundamental.

Stage 5: Identify the request assignments that ought to be practiced. Should certain assignments be done before others can be begun? Or then again can certain tasks be practiced simultaneously?

Stage 6: Identify jobs. Who will be associated with what tasks or exercises? A few assignments may include straightforward computerization apparatuses and no human endorsement, while others will require a survey and close down. Distinguish who is in charge of which assignment and procedure in your work process. Include a dip path for every job in your swimlane chart.

Stage 7: Identify your flowchart type and coax it out. Once more, swimlane charts are best for procedures, while a straightforward flowchart may work for ventures or other littler work processes. You can either coax one out by hand or utilize an apparatus like Visio, gliffy.com or draw.io.

Stage 8: Review and conclude. After you've set everything up, you will need to test your work process and audit it to guarantee that all procedures are effective and feasible and that everything achieves what it needs to achieve.

Stage 9: Use a work process computerization instrument to make your genuine work process. When your work process is settled, you can utilize work process robotization programming to set up your genuine work process and incorporate it with another programming. Remember to test your frameworks to ensure there are no hiccups all through the procedure.

When you have the flowchart, you have to make the documentation. Make a report (Word, Google Docs, whichever) and rundown out the accompanying...

Cover sheet – The title of the work process you're recording

Extension – Which groups, offices, and authority does the work process include? If the work process is for making and supporting an advertising spending plan, it could include the promoting group and CFO.

The Procedure – The accurate advances that the work process includes and the applicable chart.

Valuable Information – Any extra data on the work process.

Creating Workflow Applications

Work process improvement advances through after advances:

Plan the work process application – Before you start creating work process applications, examine the business forms that you need to computerize. Distinguish the objective of every business procedure, what its segment assignments are, and how the tasks ought to be separated into littler exercises and steps. Articulate the conditions that trigger a work process occasion and what happens when those conditions happen. Comprehend who your work process clients are and how you'll figure out who gets a work thing. As you plan the work process application, recognize the work process guidelines and how they identify with the information articles and exchanges.

Assemble the fundamental application.

Make work process maps. Use programming to make graphical maps that speak to your business procedure. At this stage, you make maps just for the procedures that are associated with the hidden application; you add work process explicit components to the maps when you characterize occasions and routings.

Characterize jobs and clients. Characterize clients' jobs when you give them their client IDs. Jobs are significant. To guarantee that work streams to the right individual, you should figure out who that individual is. You can locate the ideal individual utilizing either question jobs or client list jobs.

Make a worklist record – The worklist record figures out which fields of data the framework stores for each work thing, including the information expected to get to the objective page (the quest keys for the page) and any extra data that you need to show in the worklist itself. Since various worklist sections can have diverse objective pages and show information, you need separate worklist records for the various kinds of passages that will show up in the worklist.

Characterize work process objects – Events and routings are the two articles on the work process maps. To characterize these work process objects, add the symbols to the guide, connected to the progression speaking to the page where the activating occasion happens.

Characterize occasion triggers – After you make work process forms, interface them into the corporate applications.

Test – No advancement is finished until the work process is completely tried. Make certain to test under an assortment of conditions, both regular and irregular.

CONCLUSION

From the topics discussed above, it is understandable that there are wide possibilities for Workflow Automation. Whatever process the client is following, there is a scope of Workflow Automation in it. This helps in saving time, material, save cost and that can be effectively used for another important task for the organization.

4

RPA IN ACCOUNTS RECEIVABLE

OBJECTIVE

The objective of this chapter is to explain the importance of Oracle Receivable Module, Why this module is important for the Client's Management/Leadership team and what is the impact of delayed data input/Process delay/Manual work/any bottlenecks. How a company can increase the efficiency of processes by incorporating the Robotic Automation in their company?. Share the experience from actual Doyensys clients.

INTRODUCTION – RECEIVABLES

Receivables are the cash cow of any company. It records the revenue/Cash-in details of every sale of goods or services, which is the primary data used to calculate the profitability of the company. When you sell goods or services, the financial record is captured in the Account Receivable through an invoice or receipt of cash. Most of us understand the concept that an Invoice is created to record the Revenue and Receipt is created to record the cash. When you create an invoice, you have earned revenue but not necessarily received cash at this time (all most all companies follow accrue based accounting). The cash is identified, only after creating a receipt in the receivable module.

Apart from Invoice and Receipts, Receivable is also used to track the aging and then collections team take over to handle the delinquent customers. Other important activities include adjustments/write-offs, Print documents and closing books. All these are daily activities, and needs to be managed correctly and completed efficiently to achieve healthy cash flow to the company.

How is the data from Receivables important?

The collective sum of Receivables (which is the revenue generated and cash yet to be received), the sum of cash received, the turnover rate of the company, the Receivable ratio, etc… are some of the terminologies we hear a lot. These play a vital role in understanding how the receivable is performing, which in turn directly correlated to profitability and the overall health of the company.

Receivable records the financial transactions of a company and provides data to the key stakeholders, to understand how good their company is performing. So it is an essential financial performance indicator. If you are one of the key stakeholders of a company, then you would spend a considerably large amount of time in

➢ Understanding how your business is performing,

➢ When are we receiving the cash?

➢ Is our company in a profit category?

➢ What is the financial health of the company?

➢ How is cash flow?

➢ What is the account receivable ratio (average time to collect cash)?

➢ Where your next customer is going to come from?

➢ Are our existing customers happy with us?

➢ How many customers are delinquent?

Let us see the critical areas/rations used by companies across the globe to uncover the quality of a business's account receivable.

On-time Data Entry: It is very important for any company to record the transaction details on-time. Any delay in this causes a delay in receiving credit to the company.

Accuracy of data: Accurate data to be recorded in the system. Inaccurate data might lead to delay in credit as well because it requires more time to correct the data and then regenerate the report for analysis.

On-time Book Closing: This is another area that has significant importance. Any delay in closing the books, leads to delayed accounting of records and also next period's data entry also gets affected.

Account Receivable Ratio: Average amount of time takes to collect credit sales. An account receivable ration of 75 means, the company gets the cash on the 75th day after creating an invoice.

Receivable Turn-Over Ratio: It is the ratio of net credit sales of a given period to the average receivables received. It is an efficiency ratio that measures how efficiently a company using its assets. The accounts receivable turnover ratio measures the number of times over a given period that a company collects its average accounts receivable. Eg: If a company has an annual average of 80000 rupees and annual sales are 400000 rupees, then the Receivable Turn Over Ratio is 5 (400000/80000).

Aging Report: It is a periodic report that categorizes a company's outstanding accounts receivable invoices into different buckets. This is the primary report used by the collection team to identify defaulters.

Credit Worthiness: It helps to determine how worthy your customers to receive credit.

Faster Processing of Data: Concurrent programs or jobs related to Accounts Receivable should run very efficiently and effectively. Often time, the programs might not complete on time due to various reasons cause a delay in the recording of data. This is related to the performance of the jobs or programs that runs for Account receivable.

All of the above areas are frequent monitoring (report generation or dashboard), analyzed for its performance (review of reports), corrective actions are taken (collections, data quality issues, timely recording of transactions), and derive and implement strategies to achieve god receivable performance and the overall health of the company.

ROBOTIC PROCESS AUTOMATION IN RECEIVABLES

In the earlier session, we have discussed the importance of Account Receivable and what are the significances of various activities within Receivable that contribute to efficient cash flow to the company. One of the Boston Consulting Group Publication states that systematic incorporating the RPA into the process can increase the production of the company and also boost the ability to generate insights.

"2 of the most famous buzzword in receivable is Robotic Process Automation and Artificial Intelligence."

Now let us see how RPA can contribute to efficient receivables.

Why is RPA required for Receivables?

If you ask any anyone, they would say that the receivables module cannot function effectively without human interference. There is a lot of manual work involved in receivable activities like Data processing, Data correction, Bug fixing, Period close, generating reports, printing invoices, sending out copies to clients, collections work, generate dashboard, and many others. Most of these activities are repetitive. With the incorporation of Robotic Process Automation, these manual processes can be eliminated or reduced considerably. The time saved in using this, can be effectively utilized for other improvement activities within receivables.

Organizations should aggressively move towards business process automation for receivables to provide a cost effective operations and efficient and clean recording of data.

Below is a real use case where **_Doyensys_** has achieved Process automation in a Receivable month close. Earlier the month close was taking anywhere from 5 to 7 business days. We have identified the gap and assessed the possibility of adding automation. Post out RPA implementation, the time taken to close the period has reduced considerably to less than 2 days. The manual intervention has been considerably reduced, thereby the quality of data process skyrocketed. Below is the real time saving we have achieved.

	Without Automation (hrs)		With Automation (Hrs)
	08	Preparation for Month end like cleaning interface, etc	2
	48	Transfer Data files and loading into interface	12
MONTH CLOSE PROCESS	24	Error correction and reprocess	12
	12	Creating transactions and accounting	5
	6	Print invoices and email	2
	16	Run reports	7
	8	Identify data corruption and fix	1
	8	Closing Books	0.5

ADJUSTMENT API

Adjustment of transactions is one of the very important functions within receivable. An adjustment in Receivable means an amount added or subtracted from the balance due of an Invoice, Debit memo, Chargeback, Deposit or Guarantee.

As we know, Account Receivable holds the cash-in details to the company. The balance in this module represents the awaiting credit to the company. As per the process, some credit will never get collected or need an adjustment due to various reasons like data errors, customer disputes, or other collection-related issues. So it is essential to get the receivable adjusted so that the balance is corrected.

Typically for adjusting the transactions, companies would opt for manual adjustment for fewer adjustments, or use any third-party tools like Data loader for a large number of adjustments. But if the number of adjustments is greater than thousands then manual or data loader is not efficient. They are prone to errors and troubleshooting would take considerable amount of time. So we need a viable solution to make it more efficient and use fewer human resources. We can use RPA to automate this process, which would save more than 90%.

In Doyensys, we have suggested the RPA process for many clients that helped them in saving time and achieve a smooth and error-free day-to-day process.

Use Case – Adjustment API Program

We have developed an API program to adjust transactions for one of the largest retailing company in the world. The share service team of that client works daily to create thousands of adjustments manually. When the number of adjustments increased further, the shared service team was not able to meet the daily demand. We have identified the issue and provided a Robotic Process Automation solution that would save them enormous workforce and time.

We have started our RPA process with an analysis of the Adjustment process. We have noticed that the client's shared service team is subdivided into multiple teams, so that each of them creates adjustment with different adjustment types and with the various number of columns/DFF's. That means the number of fields used by one team is entirely different from the other team. Our initial task was to identify a common format to capture the entire data. Once the format was identified we have formulated a standard template to capture the data. Based on this template a procedure has been developed which would take the data from the template and create adjustments using an API.

The Procedure was designed to run efficiently and in less time. It has been unit tested with multiple scenarios and different unit test cases to record the performance and then it has been migrated to Production. Initially the Shared service team sends the data in the required format to the AMS team, and then the AMS team will execute the API procedure through change management process. Then later the same package has been registered as a program and given to the shared service team, so that they do not need to depend on the AMS team to execute the script.

Below is the major block of code used for the Adjustment API:

```
For i in C1 loop
            ln_ccid := null;
            v_PAYMENT_SCHEDULE_ID := null;
            v_customer_trx_id := null;
            v_segment2 := null;
    begin
        select segment2,PAYMENT_SCHEDULE_ID,rcta.customer_trx_id
            into v_segment2,v_PAYMENT_SCHEDULE_ID,v_customer_trx_id
          from apps.ra_customer_trx_all rcta
          , apps.ra_cust_trx_types_all rctta
          , apps.gl_code_combinations gcc
          , apps.ar_payment_schedules_all apsc
           where 1=1
          and rcta.trx_number = i.trx_number
          and rcta.cust_trx_type_id = rctta.cust_trx_type_id
          and rcta.customer_trx_id = apsc.customer_trx_id
```

```
            and rctta.GL_ID_REV = gcc.code_combination_id;

            exception

            WHEN OTHERS

            THEN

             DBMS_OUTPUT.PUT_LINE('Exception at trx number location
derivation'||SQLERRM);

        END;

          BEGIN

            select code_combination_id

            into ln_ccid

            from apps.gl_code_combinations

            where 1=1

            and segment1 = v_segment1

            and segment2 = v_segment2

            and segment3 = v_segment3

            and segment4 = v_segment4

            and segment5 = v_segment5

            and segment6 = v_segment6

            and segment7 = v_segment7

            and segment8 = v_segment8

            and segment9 = v_segment9;

            exception

            WHEN OTHERS

            THEN

               DBMS_OUTPUT.PUT_LINE('Unable to derive ccid'||SQLERRM);

            END;

                BEGIN
```

```
up_adj_rec.acctd_amount :=  i.adjustment_amount;

up_adj_rec.adjustment_id := null;

up_adj_rec.adjustment_number := null;

-- up_adj_rec.adjustment_type := 'M';

up_adj_rec.amount :=         i. adjustment _amount ;

up_adj_rec.created_by := 17981;-- user_id

up_adj_rec.comments := Adjustment_Fix;

up_adj_rec.created_from := 'ARXTWADJ';

up_adj_rec.creation_date := sysdate;

up_adj_rec.gl_date := trunc(to_date('01-AUG-2018','DD-
MON-YYYY'));

up_adj_rec.last_update_date := sysdate;

up_adj_rec.last_updated_by := 17981; -- User_id

up_adj_rec.set_of_books_id := 101;

up_adj_rec.code_combination_id :=ln_ccid;

up_adj_rec.status := 'A';

up_adj_rec.type := 'LINE';

up_adj_rec.payment_schedule_id :=
v_PAYMENT_SCHEDULE_ID;

up_adj_rec.apply_date := trunc(to_date('01-AUG-
2018','DD-MON-YYYY'));

up_adj_rec.receivables_trx_id := lv_receivables_trx_id;

up_adj_rec.customer_trx_id := v_customer_trx_id;


----+++--------------------------------+++---

--Calling the adjustment API ---

--+++--------------------------------+++---

 ar_adjust_pub.create_adjustment
```

```
                                        (p_api_name

=> up_api_name,

                                        p_api_version

=> up_api_version,

                                        p_init_msg_list

=> up_init_msg_list,

                                        p_commit_flag

=> up_commit_flag,

                                        p_validation_level

=> up_validation_level,

                                        p_msg_count

=> up_msg_count,

                                        p_msg_data

=> up_msg_data,

                                        p_return_status

=> up_return_status,

                                        p_adj_rec

=> up_adj_rec,

                                        p_chk_approval_limits        =>
up_chk_approval_limits,

                                        p_check_amount

=> up_check_amount,

                                        p_move_deferred_tax          =>
up_move_deferred_tax,

                                        p_new_adjust_number          =>
up_new_adjust_number,

                                        p_new_adjust_id

=> up_new_adjust_id,

                                        p_called_from

=> up_called_from,

                                        p_old_adjust_id
```

```
=> up_old_adjust_id

                                                      );

                        END;


                        commit;


            IF    up_return_status = 'S'
                  THEN
                        DBMS_OUTPUT.PUT_LINE('Discount Adjustment
Number: ' || up_new_adjust_number||' '||'Trx Number '||i.trx_number);


                        Update apps.XX_Data_Fix set status='S' where
trx_number=i.trx_number;


                  Commit;


            ELSE
                  IF up_msg_count >=1 THEN
                        FOR j IN 1..up_msg_count
                        LOOP
                        DBMS_OUTPUT.PUT_LINE('--++--------------------
----------------------++-------------');
                        DBMS_OUTPUT.PUT_LINE('Error in Transaction
:'||' '||'Trx Number '||i.trx_number);
                        DBMS_OUTPUT.PUT_LINE('Return Status -
>'||up_return_status);
                        DBMS_OUTPUT.PUT_LINE('Msg Count -
>'||up_msg_count);
                        DBMS_OUTPUT.PUT_LINE('Msg Data -
```

```
>'||up_msg_data);

                                DBMS_OUTPUT.PUT_LINE( RPAD (' ', 80, ' '));

                                DBMS_OUTPUT.PUT_LINE( RPAD ('*', 80, '*'));

                                DBMS_OUTPUT.PUT_LINE(j||'.
'||SUBSTR(FND_MSG_PUB.Get(p_encoded => FND_API.G_FALSE ), 1, 255));

                                DBMS_OUTPUT.PUT_LINE('--++--------------------
----------------------++-------------');

                            Update apps.XX_Data_Fix set status='E' where
trx_number=i.trx_number;

                                commit;

                        END LOOP;

                    END IF;

                END IF;


            END loop;
```

Results

This API program would complete in less than 30 minutes as against 20 staff-hours. This was a huge saving for the client.

ADJUSTMENT APPROVAL API

This is another API that would be very much used for most organizations. Often, the Support team receives last-minute requests to approve adjustments. Or another use case would be that if the approver is on vacation, the urgent adjustments need to be approved. If the adjustment approval process can be automated then this would save time.

Solution

While working for a client, we identified a need to create this adjustment approval API program to automate the approval process. The client used to have an approval hierarchy and they used to get last bulk adjustments and get that processed immediately.

Our team has designed a program to automatically approve the adjustments. The adjustment data will be provided to the support team in a standard template along with the regional manager's approval for approving adjustments. Then the files will be loaded on to a staging table and then the API program will be run to approve the adjustments.

```
set serveroutput on

DECLARE

v_msg_count  number(4);

v_msg_data  varchar2(1000);

v_return_status  varchar2(5);

p_count  NUMBER;

v_old_adjustment_id  ar_adjustments.adjustment_id%type;

v_new_adjustment_id ar_adjustments.adjustment_id%type;

v_adj_rec  ar_adjustments%rowtype;


CURSOR  C1  IN  select  ADJUSTMENT_ID  from  apps.ar_adjustments_all  WHERE
CREATED_BY=10001; -- Change this query to select the adjustments to be approved


BEGIN

/*-------------------------------------+

|  Setting global initialization      |

+-------------------------------------*/

FOR I in C1

LOOP

--APPS_INITIALIZE(user_id,resp_id , resp_appl_id)

FND_GLOBAL.apps_initialize(13898,50897,222);    --- user_id, responsibility_id,
module

MO_GLOBAL.init('AR');

mo_global.set_policy_context('S','101'); -- ORG
```

```
/*-----------------------------------+
|  Setting value to input parameters  |
+-----------------------------------*/
v_old_adjustment_id := I.ADJUSTMENT_ID;
v_adj_rec.type := 'LINE';
/*-----------------------------------+
|  Calling to the API           |
+-----------------------------------*/
AR_ADJUST_PUB.Approve_Adjustment(
 p_api_name => 'AR_ADJUST_PUB',
 p_api_version => 1.0,
 p_msg_count => v_msg_count ,
 p_msg_data => v_msg_data,
 p_return_status => v_return_status,
 p_adj_rec => v_adj_rec,
 p_old_adjust_id => v_old_adjustment_id);
/*-----------------------------------+
|  Error handling               |
+-----------------------------------*/
DBMS_OUTPUT.put_line('Return status ' || v_return_status );
DBMS_OUTPUT.put_line('Message count ' || v_msg_count);
IF v_msg_count = 1 Then
   DBMS_OUTPUT.put_line('l_msg_data '||v_msg_data);
ELSIF v_msg_count > 1 Then
   LOOP
     p_count := p_count+1;
```

```
    v_msg_data := FND_MSG_PUB.Get(FND_MSG_PUB.G_NEXT,FND_API.G_FALSE);

    IF v_msg_data is NULL THEN

      EXIT;

    END IF;

    DBMS_OUTPUT.put_line('Message' || p_count ||' ---'||v_msg_data);

  END LOOP;

END IF;

END LOOP;

END;

/
```

Results

By developing this program, our team was able to save hours for the business users and also saved time for the support team.

Clean audit history is maintained in an audit table, which was helpful for the Sox audit team if they needed any information. Below is the major piece of the code that was used.

MONTH END PROCESS

Month close or period close process is considered very significant for any industry. Especially when the close happens quarterly or annually, this scenario could be like a war. This month's close process involves multiple systems, many teams within shared service, Finance teams, AMS team and of course the leadership team for reporting. Each and every stage should be properly completed by each team to achieve a successful close. This also means that there are lot of dependencies with-in or outside teams and should follow a coordinated approach for a successful close.

During that close process, the Top management would be kept on looking for their email to get an update on the close period process. It involves the final transactions to be created and accounted in a very short span of time so there are lot of things that can go wrong here. Any potential delay or inaccurate data leads to delay in the close process or it causes wrong amount accounted to the receivables. This in turn affects the cash-in details and also the major reports that would be used by the leadership team.

Solution

Many companies would opt to add highly paid consultants to keep track of this process. Their job would be the monitor the process, report for any contingencies and come up with mitigation plan. It is very evident that considerable amount of time and money spent to achieve a smooth and successful close. Any savings in time on the process, would considerably benefit the company and also help to achieve an error-free and efficient close. How can we achieve this?. Let's see some of the RPA experienced by Doyensys.

Mind the Gap

All companies would have a detailed checklist of activities that need to be completed by different teams across verticals to achieve a timely and accurate close. Mostly there will be some dependency gaps in the list that would contribute to month close time.

For one of the biggest retailer has a very big checklist and the time consumed between the close activities were spanning 8 to 12 or more hours. Our team has reviewed the checklist and suggested few modification to the program. This modification is to include auto emails to concerned parties, so that they will be notified immediately to start the next one. The modification also includes generating automatic reports and emailing them to relevant parties. This simple automation in the program saved 7 hours.

Report set

Often the transaction creation program would consist of running multiple programs. If all these programs need to submitted manually one of another, then one can assume how time spent here. This becomes a very cumbersome process especially when many files to process. Instead of running manually, one of think of creating a report set would avoid this manual dependency. This will save hours of time that can be utilized for another critical month close activates.

If the submission of requests depends on complex logic, then the same automation can be achieved in the procedure as well.

Automatic File Transfer and Concurrent program execution

One of the biggest record management companies process thousands of invoices, adjustments and receipts files for month-end. They have used a third-party service to transfer the files over to Oracle and then the receivable analyst would run the transaction generation program manually in a batch-wise manner. The entire successful processing of the files would take anywhere from 4 to 6 business days.

We have identified that there are many areas with in the process has stopped. The programs to create transactions were not initiated as soon as a file arrives. Also after every batch, there is a huge pause. If we could somehow prevent these pauses, then we would be able to save least 20 % of time. This is what we have achieved. There is an automation tool called Workload automation, was used in conjunction with Oracle and third-party systems. Workload Automation tool can manage complex workloads across multiple platforms, ERP systems and many business apps. This tool is capable of transferring the files over to Oracle, then can run the concurrent programs automatically and then notify relevant parties of frequent updates. The tool will monitor the run time of the program and on successful completion it will trigger the next batch.

Error Correction

This is another major activity during the close period process. The time taken to complete this task depends on the number of errors that we receive during the process. Ideally we should not receive any errors, but often time we do due to one of the following reasons

1. Missing setups associated with new transactions

2. Data issue from the source

3. Data file issue

4. Data corruption due to process

5. Error due to manual intervention

Error Correction due to data issues from source can be fixed by incorporating controls while inputting data into the source system. This requires a careful analysis of the type of errors. These controls should be derived based on the data requirements in Oracle.

Training to the users can also help here, for example copy-pasting from Excel can cause additional characters.

Data stuck due to missing setups is mainly due to a gap in the process. Whenever any new change happens at the source, then a process should be implemented to create associated setups in Oracle before sending the actual data.

Data file issue and Data corruption due to process are mainly due to the inefficacies of jobs. The jobs should be thoroughly analyzed and checked for any gaps. Where ever possible, RPA should be implemented within the job so as avoid any manual intervention or process gaps.

In an ideal world, we will still receive some errors. This needs error correction, but we can automate the error correction process. Below is an example from a leading retail company, where we have created programs that will identify errors and correct them.

When Doyensys working for a Support project in a leading retail company, we used to receive tickets to update the gl_date of the invoice transactions that were stuck in the staging table. We used to get multiple requests per day during the close and resolving one request would take at least 2-3 hours time for the change process to complete. We identified this as a bottleneck and proactively approached client to create a concurrent program for this activity. The beauty is that this program was added to the report set of creating invoices, so while creating the invoices itself the program identifies the errors and fixes it automatically. This completely avoided the dependency with the Support Team and the client saved 8 to 10 hours to use if for other critical items.

Results

As mentioned in the solution, altogether we have saved 2-3 business days by identifying various areas of automation and incorporating RPA in it.

CREDIT MEMO API

Credit memos are created to reduce the balance of a customer. This is one of the very important activities of the shared service team.

Use Case

In couple of scenarios, we identified a need for creating an API program for credit memos. One of the scenarios is that the client's shared service team often receive request to create credit memos especially just before the month-end. Similarly the AMS team used to receive ad-hoc bulk request to create credit memos. The occurrences of these two scenarios were repetitive, so we identified a need to automate this.

We have proposed to create an API program to create the credit memos and designed a global template to handle all the columns by the organization. The program was designed in such a way to handle huge volume of records in short time and we have also incorporate to display detailed errors in the log file for easy troubleshooting. A report was also developed with the code, so that after processing the record a report is generated and can be emailed to the concerned parties if needed. Below is the piece of the code used for the program.

PURGING PROGRAMS

There is another area where RPA can be implemented, which would improve the performance of the custom program drastically. This is to purge the old data from the custom tables. Standard oracle's Archival and Purge program lets the organization periodically save and delete records from standard tables that no longer required for online. This would improve system performance.

Similarly over a period of time, data would pile up in the custom staging table and often causes the loading program to run longer due to higher SQL cost. Some organizations would design the program by thinking in advance about the volume of records that might process in the coming years.

RPA can be helpful in automatically purge data from the main staging table to an archival table.

Use case

This is specific to the organization as the custom program might have been designed to meet their internal requirement. While working for one of the leading retail giant, we had an opportunity to design a purging program that would run automatically in a schedule.

The client used to process millions of invoices in a month and each used to contain 100 or more lines. Consider storing the data in the staging table, which grow considerably in couple of years time. We have noticed the performance of the custom loading program deteriorating over time. The loading program that used to process 1000 invoices in 10 minutes to 40 minutes. This delayed the completion of further processes and it has been an escalation.

After we have developed a new program to purge the records, we let it run every weekend to delete the records from the staging table. The issue with performance has been resolved and went back to normal.

SMART PROGRAMS TO FIX BUGS

Have you ever wondered how much time are we spending to fix a data corruption in your organization? In our experience in support projects, the AMS team would spent at least 40 hours or more to resolve data fix related issues. This means that the business would be in halt until the issue is resolved.

All most all organization, would have faced standard data corruption issue. In normal scenarios, the organization would raise a ticket with Service desk and then get a fix from Oracle. After receiving the fix, the organization would test the fix in lower instance and sometimes if the corruption does not exist, then they have to clone instance freshly. The entire process would take anywhere from 2 to 5+ days to resolve the issue.

If the corruption happens during the middle on the month, then organization would not have much impact to the business. But if this corruption happens during month close or any critical process, then this would considerable impact the close process or revenue. Most of the corruption that happens in an organization would have a pattern. That means, the type of fix we execute would be similar in nature. By tracking the pattern, we would be able to identify the repetitive issues and associated fixes.

Process Automation can be very much useful in these scenarios, this would save considerable amount of time.

Use case

We have seen that the nature of corruption would be similar in nature for a particular organization. What we have seen work better, is to create a program to scan the corruption on a regular basis. After identifying the corruption, a program needs to be developed to fix the corruption issue. In general one can adopt a RPA process to identify the corruption and fix. Below are the steps in brief;

1. Identify the corruption and obtain data fix

2. Create a report program to scan data in order to identify corruption on regular basis

3. Create a fix program to correct/fix the data.

Let's see how RPA can be implemented in details

Identify the corruption and Obtain data fix

The corruption can be broadly classified into two types. They are as follow;

1. Standard Data corruption

2. Data corruption due to client-specific programs

Standard data corruption occurs during the standard process for example creating orphan events during create accounting program. This corruptions are supported by Oracle. As this corruption is repetitive in nature and since applicable to all organizations, Oracle has come up with a global data fix for these kind of standard corruptions. Look for past 1 to 2 years of issue history in any organization to come up with a list of GDF's applied to the instance.

Similarly there is another corruption of data that occurs due programs created by organization to load data into Oracle. In receivable the best example is loading flat file into oracle in order to create new invoices. During this process, data corruption may occur. And the fix to resolve this issue lies with the respective organization. Similar to Standard GDF, look for the past 2 years data and come up with a list of repetitive issues.

CREATE A REPORT TO IDENTIFY DATA CORRUPTION

This is very important in the process of RPA. If we can identify the issue as soon as it happens, then we will be able to resolve it immediately. We need not need to wait until someone finds out later.

With the identification of Standard GDF's and Organization specific fixed, we can develop a report. This report can be run any time or can be scheduled frequently to scan the errors. One important point to note here is that, the program should not take much time to complete. So it is important to analyze the cost of the queries used in the program and a sound technical person should use appropriate tuning.

Some of the major select query that can be used for any organization are mentioned below;

Program for data fix

As we know Oracle Corporation provided standard data fixes for repetitive issues that can be executed as soon as the issue has been identified. These fixes are approved by Oracle and it is called the Global Data Fixes (GDA). After receiving prior approval from the business and Oracle, we would be able to execute the data fix as a concurrent program.

Similarly many organization would load data from third-party system into oracle through interface or API. During this process, many times the data issue would occur. These also needs to be resolved as soon as possible to continue the smooth flow of data. These fixes would be custom to the process and specific to the industry. By analyzing the data corruption issue in the past two years would give us a clue about which fix is taking time to resolve. After identifying the fix

We recommend that these fixes can be clubbed together to create a master fix program, that can be used to fix the corruption. Otherwise the organization need to spent time in the change management process. It is completely with the organizations policy to decide how they want to execute the programs. It can be executed ad-hoc or can be scheduled at intervals. We have implemented this fix program for one of the fortune 500 company and we have let it run on daily basis to fix the errors.

One of the major Fortune 500 Company, had similar issue. The client used to spend close to 80 hours in total to resolve the repetitive data-related issues. After implementing the programs, the dependency was completely prevented.

SMART REPORTS

Report is a document generated from the data available in Oracle tables. Reports can be customized to extract the required data that is helpful for any purpose. A simple example is the 7 Bucket Aging report, which shows the outstanding balance of customer organized in different aging days. This report will give us an idea whether the customer is delinquent and can initiate the collections process accordingly.

Similarly, the reports can be developed to any need in the organization which can help verifying the data or process. Let's talk about RPA. How can reports help in achieving the process automation?

Data Corruption Report

We have discussed about this report in the earlier session "Smart Programs to Fix Bugs". This report will display the type of corruption and its number of transactions. Based on the errors displayed, one need to execute a fix to resolve this. This report is very useful for any organization. We strongly recommend to develop a report and schedule to run frequently.

Interface reports

We have found an opportunity with a client, who frequently raises ticket with support team to get the list of transaction stuck in the interface tables for close reconciliation. The client used to raise a low severity ticket and it will take 5 working days to get this resolved. What if we can automate this process by developing a report for the business user?. We have shared this idea to the client and they have approved it as it would avoid the dependency with the support team.

Validation reports after data import

This is another area where lot of things get messy. And most cases we would only identify missing data after many weeks or only during reconciliation. Normally this validation will be performed by the business user or support person. This validation process is very tedious and many things can go wrong here.

One of the top retail company uses excel sheets, macros and formula's to validate this. First they would get the required data from Oracle by raising multiple tickets with support team. Then later they will copy the data and convert into a designated format. After that, they would compare data using many formulas and finally they will come up with the validation results. One can easily see the time delay and complexity that happens here.

Doyensys has identified an automation in this area, to take care of the entire data extraction, conversion and validating using a report. We have created a report for this and delivered it to the business user. To the organization's surprise, it eased the business user's work and saved approximately 8 to 10 hours a week.

RECEIVABLE RECEIPTS

Receipts creation, Receipt application and Receipt Write-off's are important functions within receivables. These activities convert the receivable to cash account. So these activities should be carried out with utmost efficiency and accuracy. Any delay in this, might cause the recognition of cash which in-turn affects the cash and customer aging.

Receipts creation & Application

Receipts can be created in oracle using following methods

    a. Manual
    b. Automatic through Interface
    c. Automatic through Lockbox
    d. API

Most companies uses above methods of receipt creation, and each of them has its own pros and cons. RPA can be implemented for each of the methods in some form.

Receipt Adjustments using write-offs

Most organization prefer adjustments performed manually. But as the volume increases, manual adjustments create load onto the shared service team. This is another area where RPA can be implemented.

Any savings in time by implementing the RPA would benefit the organization in a big way. Some of the use cases of RPA are discussed below;

Master API Program

For couple of Fortune 500 companies, Doyensys identified a need for a master API program. The client used to get ad-hoc requests to create, reverse, modify and adjust receipts very frequently. Every month the support team used to get 10 requests and each request would take at least 3 days to complete.

Based on the business requirement, we have created an API program with the below Oracle Standard API;

- AR_RECEIPT_API_PUB.CREATE_CASH
- AR_RECEIPT_API_PUB.APPLY
- AR_RECEIPT_API_PUB.CREATE_AND_APPLY
- AR_RECEIPT_API_PUB.UNAPPLY
- AR_RECEIPT_API_PUB.APPLY_ON_ACCOUNT
- AR_RECEIPT_API_PUB.UNAPPLY_ON_ACCOUNT
- AR_RECEIPT_API_PUB.REVERSE
- AR_RECEIPT_API_PUB.ACTIVITY_APPLICATION
- AR_RECEIPT_API_PUB.ACTIVITY_UNAPPLICATION
- AR_RECEIPT_API_PUB.CREATE_MISC
- AR_RECEIPT_API_PUB.UNAPPLY_OTHER_ACCOUNT
- AR_RECEIPT_API_PUB.APPLY_OPEN_RECEIPT
- AR_RECEIPT_API_PUB.UNAPPLY_OPEN_RECEIPT
- AR_RECEIPT_API_PUB.CREATE_APPLY_ON_ACC

We have designed the program in such a way that the mapping of data is handled outside of the code, so that in the future any changes can be performed through a form. Excel templates has been designed for each of the API, and handed over to business. The program also generates a report and email to the user for validation. This program benefited the client and achieved enormous time savings.

LOCKBOX CLEANING

Lockbox is a service provided by banks so that customer can deposit payment directly into the customer account. On a periodic basis, bank will send a lockbox file to Oracle. This file is loaded into the receipt interface table and then standard lockbox program is run to create the receipts.

For organizations who uses the lockbox functionality can follow RPA to speed up the recording of receipts in oracle.

Stuck Post Quick Cash

Often time, receipts might get stuck at the post quick cash table. Apart from affecting cash, this stuck data will not allow the period to be closed. So it is very important to clear the data as soon as possible. Below is the update statement that needs to be executed to reprocess the data.

```
UPDATE ar_batches_all

SET request_id = null,

    batch_applied_status = 'POSTBATCH_WAITING',

    status = 'OP',

    operation_request_id = null

WHERE batch_id = '12345';
```

If the above statement needs to be executed through a standard change management process, it would take at least couple of hours to resolve this issue. But it can create a program to update the batches, then that would save time. If the organization do not want to create a program for this and is okay to get this query pre-approved, then that also is a kind of RPA.

Delete Data from Interface table

This is also another possible RPA that can be implemented in organization that requires deletion of data from the interface table. This is often required especially when duplicate files loaded onto the interface table. While creating the program following points needs to be considered.

1. Always take a back of the data before deletion. Create an audit table, and insert the records before deletion.
2. Make sure the entire batch records are not processed in case of duplicate issue.
3. Make sure to delete the record from AR_TRANSIMISSIONS_ALL & AR_BATCHES_ALL TABLE, so that the transmission data will not show in the lockbox form.

Delete Duplicate Receipts

Sometimes the lockbox process creates duplicate receipts in Receivables. If the combination of Receipt Number, Amount, Currency, Customer Number and Batch are different, then in such cases lockbox will create duplicate receipts in the system.

In this case, reversing the receipt is the only option as most cases deletion is not allowed if the receipts were posted to GL. Reversing the receipts can be easier if we have an API program readily available in receivables. Please refer the section "Receivable Receipts" for the API Program.

DELETE DATA FROM STAGING OR INTERFACE TABLE

Oracle has provided ways to create transactions through interface table. If we use interface table, the standard program will validate and create transactions as per the oracle standards. The records created would be supported by oracle.

But before inserting the records into the interface table, there should be a first cut of validation performed by the organization. Ideally the data from any third party source would be inserted into a staging table first. Then the records are fetched from the staging table and validated before inserting into the interface table. Sometimes the mandatory data for interfacing is derived from the available data through the organization's specific requirement.

During the import process the records can get corrupted or the data derived wrongly due to bad data or can be loaded duplicate. So we need an efficient way of deleting data from the staging or interface table. RPA can be used here to achieve time savings.

Deletion from staging table

Based on an identified need in a customer project, we have designed a program to delete data from their staging table. The shared service team loads the data into the staging table by manually placing the file and then run the import jobs. Sometimes the files get loaded twice or incorrectly or due to delay in processing file some of the invoices will be created manually. This used to happen repetitively due to manual error. We have suggested an automated way of handling the file movement, but until the budget was allocated we have provided them a program to delete the staging records.

The input parameter to delete the record is the file_name and org_id. The program that we have designed will do the following

1. Run a validation and make sure all or part of invoices created in the receivables. If it fails the validation, deletion will not allowed.
2. Keep track of the deleted records in the audit table.
3. Send email to the user's manager with a report of deletion.

Data Deletion from Interface table

One of the leading retail company, uses WebADI to load the invoices and receipts. The shared service team get the input data from third-party systems through an email and it will copied on to the excel template for WebADI. On many occasions, they end up with unwanted lines in the interface tables. This was due to discarding data that were loaded earlier due to corruption or data error.

For this scenario, the shared service team used to create many tickets a day to the support team for deletion.

We have identified a need for automation here, so that the shared service team can save more than 4 hours for a ticket and avoids any dependency. We have designed and delivered program to delete the records by the combination of source, org_id, transaction number, date and customer.

ORACLE ALERTS

Alerts are used to inform the intended parties about any changes in the database or inform about any critical activity or share information be created in Oracle.

- ➢ Event alert
- ➢ Periodic alert

Event alert functions as an informer, where it informs or notifies the owner of any activity occurs. This alert is triggered when some change in data occurs at the database. A specific SQL statement can be written to check specific database table and based on the results, the alert can take action. Oracle has provided 4 standard actions that can be used for alerts.

1. Concurrent program
2. Message
3. Operating system script
4. SQL statement script

Similarly, a periodic alert checks the database on a schedule for specific information and based on that it can perform actions like sending data in an email

This is an oracle standard function that can be utilized for achieving automation in oracle. Some of the activities that we have performed for clients are an example of RPA in Receivables.

Adjustment Approval

Adjustment approval is widely used across the organization to control and validate the adjustments or write-offs to the transactions. This approval has to be completed before the period close activity otherwise it will be a blocker. For one the major retail company, this was a critical issue. The client often used to receive lot of approvals and sometimes the approvals were not approved on time causing delay in the close process. To fix the issue, we have created a period alert that scans for pending approval in intervals and then send a list of adjustments to be approved to the business users. This alert was a timesaver to the business users and helped to achieve 100% period close.

Alert to run concurrent program

For another client, we have identified a need to spawn a program after performing some validation. During the billing process, the client has a step to execute a report that sends emails to the third party with the invoice PDF copy. But before sending the invoice copy, there are some validations that will be performed outside of oracle. We have identified a need to automate this, so we have created a function to validate the activity and if the validation is success then the alert will trigger the invoice print and emailing program.

This automation eliminated the manual dependency completely.

MONTH CLOSE DASHBOARD

Month close is a very important activity for any organization. Especially when it comes to receivable module, it was like a war room during the close process. The importantly; the on-time closure and recording of all transaction in receivable is of paramount importance, as it affects the revenue and aging.

During the close process, major stakeholders would constantly look for continuous update from the closing team and support team on blocker issues. A considerable amount of time is spent in preparing the data for update. And there is a dependency with various teams and process to get latest information. Most the data will be gathered and compiled in a representation format manually. An automated way would definitely add value to all organization. Below is an example of one of the RPA we have designed internally.

Apex Dashboard

This was an internal project initially and then later it was deployed to couple of our clients.

While working for a major retail giant, we identified an RPA possibility in the close process. The analyst who prepares the documentation of close process spends at least 3 hours to prepare the update email for close. Similarly the analyst has to send similar updates once in every 8 hours. Sometimes the due to delay in getting the data from the respective team, causes missing/incorrect information in the updates. To support the close team, we have worked out a beautiful dashboard which shows the following information in a one-page screen.

1. Global map with close status
2. Progress of close activities with details
3. Critical issues that was created in the incident management tool
4. Any data corruption in oracle table.

Data to display above information will be fetched automatically from oracle/incident management/third party tables via apex jobs or API or scripts.

SHARED SERVICE

Shared service team's function is integral to any organization for timely recording of data into Oracle receivables. They would perform many manual tasks on a daily basis. As the tasks are mainly completed manually, there is a more chance to errors. During such cases, they would depend on AMS support team to resolve the issue.

Use case:

What we have seen is the Shared Service team has often loaded with heavy work and most times they used to extend their hours of work during the weekend to complete the work.

In one of the AMS project, past 6-month ticket analysis showed a trend of many tickets from the Shared Service team. It seems to coincide with the increase in volume of transactions. When we analyzed the issue in detail, we noticed the shared service team worked extended hours to create manual credit memos and Receipts. In order to reduce the number of inflow tickets and as to help the Shared Service team, we have proposed an automated solution to create adjustments and Credit memo's using WebADI.

Similarly for another client, we have proposed a new program to create adjustments. For that client, the volume of receipt creation was a high volume tasks. So we have designed a concurrent program to create receipts using API. We have also defined a standard template for the shared service team to input the data. Introduction of this program given them back couple of hours per resource per day, which can be utilized for other critical tasks.

ACCOUNT RECEIVABLE SWEEPING

All organization must have gone through Data corruptions during month close and they understand how time-consuming to get a data fix. Until the issue is resolved the close process needs to wait. Oracle Receivable will not allow the period to be closed if it identifies a data corruption that belong to the current open GL Period. That time the only option is to get a fix from Oracle support or get a sweep query from oracle support. Both case, time is involved.

We have gone through the same issue multiple times and worked with oracle to get a fix. But if the corruption happens during last minute and if the value of the impacted transaction is less, then the best option is to sweep that transaction to the next period and close current period. Earlier we used to work with Oracle to get a sweeping script. But the same script cannot be used for another transactions or in the future. Our internal team can develop such a script, but the organization policies will not allow to execute fix on standard tables without Oracle's blessing. So each time when it occurs, we had to work with Oracle Support.

The Oracle Fix for Sweep

Oracle has noticed the repetitive requests from many organizations and they identified a need of having a sweep facility for Receivables modules just like Oracle Payables. Oracle has incorporated this functionality lately and most organizations might be aware of this function.

In order to sweep the Receivables transition, a function called "AR_ARXSUMPS_MANAGE_EXP (Accounting Exception: Manage)"should be added to the responsibility (Oracle, 2016) that is used for closing the period. Oracle has released patch to add this particular function and then the organization need to add this function to the required responsibility.

- For R 12.1, apply Patch 18798268 or through AUG-2014 RPC Patch 19125641
- For R 12.2, apply Patch 16634326

After applying the patch, a button "Manage Exception" will be displayed on the close screen. During close if receivable identifies any unaccounted distributions, then we can review the affected records by clicking Manage Exception button, which will open a pop-up window like below;

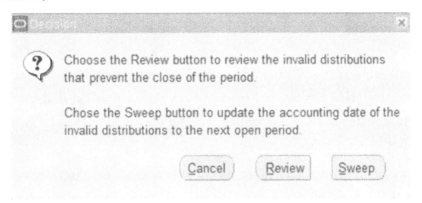

We can choose to review the transactions then click on Sweep button. This will spawn concurrent program "Unaccounted Transaction Sweep" to sweep the transaction to the given GL Period.

This is a very useful functionality for Receivables. But always please make sure to review the transactions for before initiating the sweep.

CHAT BOT

Chatbot is trending tool which was designed to replace the human with computer for chatting. It is an Artificial Intelligence tool capable of learning from mistake and it is evolving day by day. It is tool very much used in the customer service area and to gather information. Most organization developed and delivered the chatbot for outside organization communications. The same tool also can be used in the internal organization as well.

One such need is evolving in the area of AMS support. One can think of developing a smart Chatbot that can help the organizations internal needs. One such example is that many times the support team receives process-related questions in a support ticket. The process documents might be available in some shared location, but the user might not be aware of that. Such cases can be easily handled using a ChatBot.

WHAT IS ALEXA?

Today the world is exploring the possibility of using virtual assistants in each and every tasks. All major leading companies in the world are exploring the virtual space and few companies has already became a leader. Amazon is one such company who has developed a virtual assistants and artificial intelligence tool named as "Alexa". Alexa uses Natural Language Processing (NLP) to convert speech into words, sounds and ideas. Alexa is being there close to two years now and it is getting smarter day by day. The ability to handle tasks on command is ever-expanding.

This virtual assistance can listen to human speech, recognize what it heard and perform the actions asked by the user. With the addition of internet and API, the virtual assistance can connect to any software and get the task done. Its usage is very much popular at home to control the products like switching lights, turning on/off TV, listen to music, so on and so forth.

When we ask Alexa to complete any tasks, Alexa uses internet to connect to the "Alexa Voice Services (AVS)" by internet and then the voice heard is send over to the AVS for interpretation. After understanding the tasks, AVS send information to Alexa device to perform (Gonfalonieri, 2018).

Alexa with Oracle

While working in support projects for multiple global clients, we often get requests from the business users to perform some simple tasks in oracle. In order to complete the simple tasks, the user needs to raise a ticket and wait for day or two to get their action completed. Similarly, the senior management team also asks for certain data, for which they had to wait for hours to get that completed. One such example is to get the open balance for a customer.

At Doyensys, we have identified a need to automation here by incorporating any intelligent tool to complete the tasks. Out internal team has explored the possibility of using Alexa with oracle and they have succeeded.

We have integrated Alexa with Oracle. When we ask how many orders are created for a customer in oracle, the Alexa will connect to Oracle, then execute a query, fetch the number of orders and then speak using the speaker. After asking the question, the answer is heard within few seconds. There is no limit to the capability of Alexa, we only need to think about the usage and then implement it. Some of the tasks that can be completed in receivables using Alexa as follow

> Invoice balance
> Total Outstanding Balance of a customer
> Check receipt status
> Close status
> Execute a program
> Orphan record count

We also showed a Demo at SANGAM18 event and many clients were interested in using Alexa for tasks in oracle.

AGING PROCESS

Aging is an important process followed by all organizations. Aging is nothing but categorizing the outstanding balance of the customers in different buckets of ages. This is primarily used by the collections team to identify which invoices are due for payment. Based on the identification, the collection team would initiate the collections process by emailing or contacting customers to collect the payment.

Other important details provided by aging would help the management in planning and implementing strategies are as follows

> Determine financial health of the company
> Identify irregularities
> Identify bad debt
> Calculate credit risk
> Identify delinquent customers

Dashboard

Aging is closely associated with the collections team. At the same time, one can see the importance of aging report to the key management people. In our experience, any delay in the collections process is considered very critical for the collection team. And it is even more critical for the management people.

They need to have the up to date information of the aging with them to strategize plans for their company in order improve the % of outstanding balance and thereby improving the overall health of the company. Majority of the time, the management team would be dependent on the Collections team or AMS Support team for the data. It will be wonder if we can provide a dashboard for the management team with the help of Oracle Apex.

We identified the need of a dashboard and it is in progress. The dashboard is being developed with Oracle Apex and it displays all relevant information displayed for the management. Up-to-date data will be refreshed almost real-time and it can be extended to a mobile app as well.

CONCLUSION

From the real use cases discussed above, it is understandable that there is wide possibilities of Robotic Automation in Oracle Module. Whatever process the client is following, there is a scope of automation in it. This helps in saving time and that can be effectively used for other important task for the organization. With our experience with various clients, we will be able to implement 20 to 40% automation that could save at least 20 hours.

RECOMMENDATIONS

Below are some of the recommendations from Doyensys based on our work experience with various clients.

- ➢ Oracle has provided various Application Process Interfaces (API) to create or modify transactions. Use this API effectively by creating a program, so that day to day business activities can be handled through it rather than taking manual approach.
- ➢ Analyze the long-running concurrent programs and understand which query is consuming more time (by tkprof). Work with Oracle to rectify the issue or enforce the best SQL plan

➢ Purge records that are no longer needed as per the business and SOX requirement. Clean up the customer table created, as this is one of the major reason for performance issues

➢ Create a standalone or multiple programs to fix the repetitive issues that occurs day in and day out.

➢ Create a concurrent program for executing Global Data Fixes. This is required especially for the month-end and save time.

SUMMARY (SHORT OVERVIEW)

Receivable module is one of the important modules used by the client leadership team to understand the cash flow.

Any potential delay in the transaction creation causes delay in generating reports which in turn affects the cash flow

On-time completion of collection activities is must to take care of the customers and their aging. This is also directly correlated to the revenue

RPA can be implemented for any processes. RPA helps in preventing errors and saves time that can be used for other important tasks.

RPA IN PAYABLES

OBJECTIVE

Objective of this chapter is to explain the importance of Oracle Payables Module, Why Payables module is important in oracle to maintain the vendor payment and invoice processing to the Client's Management/Leadership team and what is the impact of delayed invoice processing and payment processing to the vendors. How do we increase the productivity of processes by incorporating the RPA in their business process?.

INTRODUCTION – PAYABLES

The Accounts Payable (AP) module is used to administer payment for products or services while preventing double payment. The module contains detailed history of accounts, giving vendors the background required to resolve issues and improve flow of goods and payments.

Apart from Invoice and Payments, Payables is also used to track the aging/ outstanding payables to the multiple vendors and then and then forecasting the company cash reserve position and based on that company can come up with new strategies of payables processing.

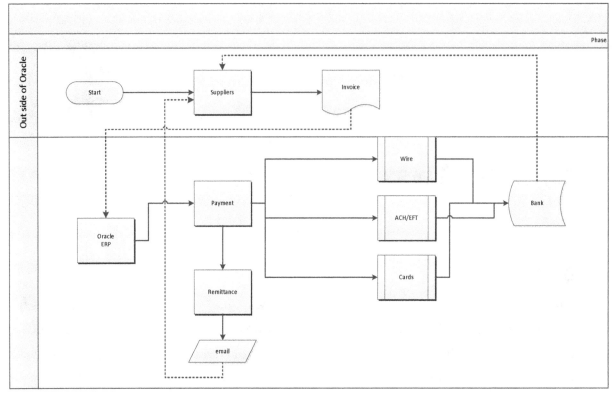

With the Accounts Payable module you can:

- Automate the approval for invoices
- Grow vendor relations with valuable historical data
- Automatically create letters for vendors who have not supplied Tax Identification numbers
- Alert when a potential duplicate invoice has been approved
- Track against prepayment and recurring payment options

Vendor Information

Maintain vendor sites and contacts with key vendor information. We can define vendor holds by invoice amount or product matching criteria. We can create a Vendor Hierarchy for easy maintenance

Recurring Payments

Set up automatic payments without processing invoices. Handles unique payment options such as balloon payments. Payments can cross over accounting periods

Automatic Interest Invoices

Payables creates the interest % required for late payment of invoices. Review online the interest payments or report on them

Invoice Import

Integration with Oracle Project Accounting or other accounting systems will allow automatic import of expense reports or invoices. Exception handling manages errors thus controlling incorrect invoices being created

How is the data from Payables important?

Payables data is more important, as the payments can be released to the vendors on time will be done by payables team. If we did not make the payment on time to the vendors, we won't be able to maintain a good relationship or the goodwill for the business and also it will backfire the total manufacturing department if we did not receive the goods from the supplier.

AP teams seem to be already working under extreme pressure to be doing more with less. As invoice volumes increase, their invoice processing is projected to grow equally more complex. In fact, percent of AP professionals reported that their total invoices have seen an increase of as much as 10 percent over the past year. AP teams from companies of all sizes have reported spending approximately half of their time dealing with transaction processing.

Centralizing accounts payable processing and reporting across the enterprise through a shared service environment to ensure all staff members adhere to common practices and standards and measure their performance against established business metrics. This has the added advantage of enabling by the company to accomplish more tasks in a faster timeframe and with fewer resources, ultimately reducing enterprise costs.

ROBOTIC PROCESS AUTOMATION IN PAYABLES

In the earlier session we have discussed about importance of Account Payables and what are the significance of various activities within Payables that contribute to an efficient cash flow to the company. One of the Boston Consulting Group Publication[1] states that by systematic incorporating the RPA into the process can increase the production of the company and also boost the ability to generate insights.

An effective accounts payable team harnesses the power of RPA to become an intelligence hub for the business and increase its strategic performance

Now let us see how RPA can contribute an efficient Payables.

Why is RPA required for Payables?

If you ask any anyone, they would say that Payables module cannot run effectively without any manual interference. There are lot of manual work involved in the Payables process like invoice processing, invoice validation, holds releasing, payment holds, code combinations fixing, Period close, generating reports, printing invoices, making payments, sending out payment copies (remittance) to the vendors and bank to make the payment on behalf us to the supplier.... Most of these payables activities are repetitive in nature like invoice processing and payment processing. With the incorporation of Robotic Process Automation, these manual process can be eliminated or reduced considerably. The time saved in using this, can be effectively utilized for other improvement activities within Payables application.

We had a business case where we have achieved Process automation in Payables month close. Initially one of our prestigious client has issues during the close time, this client was running business around the globe. Period close is the major and key area for any client, business would like to close the periods/business on time. Due to some data corruptions, bugs, user mistakes, may lead to delay in books close. With the period close issues application support team hitting with the last moment issues or the follow-ups/escalations to close all the issues which has been raised by the business, but it is not possible to work on all the issues and all resources will be blocked because of these issues and they are not able to concentrate on any other issues. Hence, they are also getting prioritized as per the SLA. Due to that month close was taking anywhere from 5 to 7 business days (means it is also getting delayed). We had implemented a plan to do the mock close process in place to avoid this issue and it has worked for 40 to 50 % of deadlines but still we did not reach the 100%. We have struggled a lot and then we come up with an idea of automation. Post out RPA implementation, there was a drastic change, team is identifying the issues and fixing them proactively before the business starts raising the issue... Manual intervention has been considerably reduced.

We have come up with a Diagnostic analyzer as a concurrent program to identify the issues at the OU level, when we have multiple operating units. In addition, we are going in detail at the transaction level issues/corruptions and master data level issues proactively.

Below are the programs that can help us to get the Diagnostics on the issues, which are there in the system currently. Please go through the oracle note on How to Register the Master GDF Diagnostic (MGD) as a Concurrent Program (Doc ID 1361255.1)

The first program will allow you to schedule and run a concurrent process, which will scan all transactions in a date range within specified operating units for any data integrity issues. The second concurrent program will allow you to specify an individual invoice, check and/or supplier ID for validation.

1. AP Data Validation Analyzer
2. AP Single Transaction Data Validation Analyzer

Example: it is to enable running the date range version of the process for multiple operating units (OU's). By default the value set for the operating unit parameter allows you to select a single OU, or leave the parameter blank (resulting in the process running for ALL OU's). When the process is run directly in SQL, however, a list of specific OU's can be provided, and some customers may require this ability when running the process as a concurrent program.

This can be accomplished by modifying the value set for the Operating Unit parameter in the "AP Data Validation Analyzer" (APGDFVAL) so that the parameter accepts free text.

Once these Programs registered in application, we will be able to get the all issue details/ or the transactions which are affected. Based on that either we can work with oracle to get the solution proactively from the oracle application. It also help us to keep the system up to date by knowing all these bugs and fixing proactively. After having these programs, team is to run these programs to knowing the issues which are there currently, based on that team can apply the GDF's for the standard oracle bugs to fix the issue and the analysis time has drastically been changed.

WHAT IS WEB ADI AND HOW IT CAN BENEFIT THE CLIENT

Web ADI that being used within the E-Business Suite to provide end-users with a familiar user interface. Web ADI is a web-based browser application (Oracle Application Framework) which helps in integrating the desktop applications MS Word, MS Excel with Oracle E-Business. WebADI increases the productivity as the user need not change the user interface which are familiar to the user. Key end-users are highly accepted this productive tool, because of their own advantages and great office capability.

ADI stands for Applications Desktop Integrator which was supported for the oracle e-business suite version 11i. This is an Excel-based interface through which users can upload and view data in the Oracle system. The users with their standard Oracle User name, and password details can access database. Web ADI is a Browser-based application, which enables users to log in to the Oracle Database, and upload ADI spreadsheets, without having to have the ADI application loaded locally on the users machine, or having it set up on a central server and users accessing it through Citrix.

User is signed into Oracle Applications in the browser. Business will click on a link that calls the Application Service showing all or part of the Create Document Page. Once all of the required information for generating a Desktop Application document has been supplied the Application Service calls off to the Document Service to start the creation process. Once generation is complete a call may be made to the Download service to retrieve any data that will be displayed in the document.

Once in the document, the user can start working with the data. Performing Data Entry, referencing to and from other documents. Where a List of Values has been enabled, calls are made to the component service to display and return data. The download service can be called again to refresh the data. When ready, the Upload service is called, passing the upload parameters and the data from the sheet encoded in an XML document, where it is processed, validated and uploaded into the database.

a. Web ADI Support for all E-business Suite certified browsers that mean you use Netscape, Mozilla and Firefox with all other self-service applications.
b. Layout Definition Enhancements, this simply means further customize your spreadsheets and Formulas
c. Add extra logic to the spreadsheet to support more user-friendly
d. Can manage large amounts of data, Can manage multiple Worksheets
e. Logically separate data for update, analysis, and distribution.

MASTER DATA CONVERSION DATA THROUGH WEBADI

We can use WEB Application desktop integrator for master data creation. If we have daily feed from business on the supplier, supplier site and supplier contacts creation. For example, daily business users are having supplier creation for any invoice processing for vendors, they can utilize this simple and user-friendly automation. If business want to use manual data entry and it may consume lot of time and resource for master data processing. Hence, we can choose the WEBADI, which is a user-friendly application for data migration to oracle application.

Supplier data is very crucial for the payables module in oracle applications. Supplier's data is divided into three parts.

1. Suppliers

2. Supplier site

3. Supplier contacts

Suppliers/ Vendors: Normally supplier's data is the key data for any payables activity. For any new implementation or rollout, we use the conversion, which is an automation for the suppliers creation. Which means, instead of creating suppliers manually we can use the oracle API's to automate the suppliers creation.

Suppliers are the key to the business, these suppliers are the people who will provide us the goods as requested and we will be making payment to them for that service rendered. In oracle applications, suppliers are the global and the supplier sites are the operating unit specific. Hence supplier might be available and visible in all ou's but the supplier site need to create for each country/operating unit separately..

We have many API's to automate the supplier's creation and management:

- API to Create Supplier - pos_vendor_pub_pkg.create_vendor
- API to Create Supplier Site - pos_vendor_pub_pkg.create_vendor_site
- API to create Supplier contact: AP_VENDOR_PUB_PKG.Create_Vendor_Contact
- AP_VENDOR_PUB_PKG.update_vendor_public API

These are the API which will be used to reduce the manual work and automate the supplier's creation, supplier site, contacts, supplier addresses, which is a onetime activity during the implementation time. Also, we may get daily supplier data, if we are using any third party or legacy systems to maintain the suppliers master data, we can use this API's converted into the programs to manage daily suppliers/vendors data..

1. Suppliers Creation: suppliers are called as vendors, with whom we are dealing/transacting with services and goods. Suppliers are at the global/instance level.

   If we want to use customized WEBADI for the supplier master data, it consists of the below steps.

   a. Create staging table where we will be loading the data for validation

   b. Define package/build code, we do have a standard API for supplier creation, we can use the same for the supplier creation through WEBADI with small changes.

   c. Define a custom integrator for Supplier creation

➢ WEBADI integrator defines all information that we need to download or upload the data from the application for a specific purpose. In this example, we are using this integrator for the supplier creation.

➢ In Supplier creation WEBADI, Layout design also plays a key role as we need to decide what fields need to be displayed for the supplier migration.

➢ Mapping needs to be done between source columns and target columns to facilitate the download of content to the desktop.

2. Supplier sites: supplier sites are the locations from where we are receiving invoices or we are making payments to the supplier sites. In oracle applications, sites will be different for each country. One supplier can have multiple sites for each location based on the business needs. For supplier sites also, we are using the same process as suppliers

   a. Staging table creation for data loading

   b. We have a separate standard API for Supplier sites which we will be using for this WEBADI

   c. We need to define a new integrator for the supplier sites, integrator is unique and it will be separate for each activity/process.

   d. Layout need to customize for the supplier sites based on the columns required.

   e. Mapping needs to be done between source columns and the target columns need to be processed.

3. Supplier contacts: supplier contacts are also playing a key role to maintain the customer address details to communicate on regular basis. This is a part of the supplier creation, which is a mandatory part before we process any invoice processing. When we make any payment, we used to send separate remittance advice to the suppliers based on this supplier contacts to inform him, for which invoice we made a payment, when we had done payment, how much we paid all these information will be send to the suppliers. Hence supplier contacts are also very much important. so we need to consider the supplier sites also for vendor master data migration.

   a. Custom table need to be created. This custom table is needed for validating the data before it moves to the standard interface table, hence it is more important.

  b. We have standard API, which need to have minimal changes for contacts loading.

  c. As the WEBADI integrator is unique for each activity, we need to define a separate integrator.

Once we load the data to the stage tables from there oracle has provided us the standard programs for importing suppliers, supplier sites and supplier contacts to the base tables. We need to run the below programs/jobs to import the master data into the base tables.

  a. To import the supplier headers information we need to run the "Suppliers open interface import"

  b. To import the supplier sites information we need to run the "Supplier sites open interface import"

  c. To import the supplier contacts information we need to run the "Suppliers contacts open interface import"

4. Master Data Migration through WEBADI Cons:

  a. It requires internal development and testing is needed before it handover to business.

  b. List of values very difficult to build

  c. It may get impacted/affected by the patching or upgrade.

5. Master Data Migration through WEBADI Pros:

  a. No need of any separate license

  b. Specific to business needs

  c. Simple user interface

  d. Time-saving and resource consumption reduced

  e. Suitable for the mid-scale clients

We had designed and developed for one of our client from people tech group and they were happy. When we compare with other developments or any other tools very cheaper and time saver. Can be used by all the users, don't have any user-specific access, anyone can use it with the help of responsibility provided.

SUPPLIER BANK ACCOUNT CREATION API

Once the suppliers and supplier sites are created in oracle application, if we want to do the electronic payments to the suppliers, supplier bank account information is a mandatory information that are required. EFT payment instruction will be sent to the suppliers. Based on the supplier request, we also can do the EFT payment, we will assign the Electronic Fund transfer payment method (EFT) to the supplier. For the EFT payment, we will create the payment file from the oracle application and system will create a payment file and the same will be sent to the internal bank for releasing the payment.

Payment file contains the supplier information and the required destination bank account details, payee bank, payee address, payee name, invoice number, payment amount, currency, internal bank/source bank...etc. . All these information will be there in the payment file and by using those details, bank will be sending the payments to the suppliers.

After the Supplier or Supplier Site is validated and a row entered in the various AP and HZ tables, a Payee is created in IBY (the new Payments application) for the Supplier or Supplier Site. If the Payee is successfully created, we then check to see if there are any corresponding rows in IBY_TEMP_EXT_BANK_ACCTS. If there are, we call an IBY API to create the Bank Account and associate it with the Payee. So to import supplier bank accounts during Supplier and Supplier Site Open Interface, you can populate the IBY_TEMP_EXT_BANK_ACCTS table.

The supplier bank account information is in the table: IBY_EXT_BANK_ACCOUNTS, the bank and bank branches information is in the table HZ_PARTIES.

Creating a supplier in AP now creates a record in HZ_PARTIES. In the create Supplier screen, you will notice that Registry_id is the party_number in HZ_Parties.

The table hz_party_usg_assignments table stores the party_usage_code SUPPLIER, and also contains the given party_id for that supplier. Running this query will return if customer was a SUPPLIER.

In order to load Supplier external bank, branches and bank accounts, one needs to use the Oracle Supplied Package IBY_EXT_BANKACCT_PUB.

INVOICE AUTOMATION WITH WEBADI

In Oracle Application or in any ERP we can have two types of Data entry to application, one could be manual entry by the end-user and it could be manual data entry and a time-consuming process… we do have another process that is, we can programmatically load the data into the oracle applications/ERP. When you choose programmatic option, you would be having data file, which you would have received from the legacy system or the file will be prepared by the business users to accomplish the program needs. When you say programmatically also, we can have two types, they are WEBADI or another one is a complete custom program which can directly place the data into interface tables with proper validations.

WEBADI stands for Web Applications Desktop Integrator; Web ADI is a most popular desktop conversant tool. Oracle E-Business Suite to the desktop where familiar desktop tool like Excel can be used to create spreadsheet, Business users can enter and edit data in the spreadsheet and finally upload the data into the Oracle Applications with the validations. Web ADI can be very useful for the users who are experienced with Excel/spreadsheet and will like to use Excel to enter the data related to Oracle Applications. Business users can increase their productivity by using WEBADI.

By using we are integrating oracle applications modules with the spreadsheet for data entry.. we do have a couple standard WEBADI's which are provided by the oracle with the product itself, but when any requirement comes for AP invoice creation automatically by using WEBADI in Oracle payables, we can customize with the minimal setups.

We can create our own integrator for payables and we can assign it to a specific responsibility, here we can't download the WEBADI template for all the data from single responsibility, we have to use specified responsibility to download the same..

We can customize WEBADI layout as per the business requirement, if we have any DFF values, we can enable to use by the business users to fill the excel template.

Benefits by Payables Invoice Processing Automation

a. It is user-friendly interface and easy to handle

b. As the layout/template looks like an excel template, business can use the same copy, paste, other features of excel.

c. It will reduce the time consumption when compared to the manual data entry

d. WEBADI is a interface validations are user-specified validations, during upload of the data, user can specify for validation and data import

e. By using WEBADI, we can also, call journal import, by selecting journal import, so no need to submit another journal import to import the data.

f. Productivity of the AP team will get improved a lot and it has been proved by many clients.

g. We had proposed this option to one of our prestigious client and the same has been implemented. Data Quality will be improved

h. We can save money by reducing the manual work and we can use the resources effectively

i. Business users no need to depend on the IT, More transparent and user can control it by himself.

j. We don't need any other ERP tools as the oracle itself have capability to integrate… no need of any third party tools..

k. No need of any separate license for WEBADI as it is included in the Financial product itself

WEBADI has some Cons

a. Long-winded development & Design process

b. Requires maintenance/Patching, when we move the form to higher version, it may come up with new field or any changes, then we need to change the WEBADi.

c. Requires minimal technical expertise as we need to build the simple queries

d. Difficult to debug

e. WEBADI can't satisfy All business expectations. It's a very basic user interface

Customizing WEBADI:

> There are few steps involved in customizing the WEB Application desktop integrator to accomplish our business requirements. Below are the steps to be considered for the new WEBADI customization.

> There are couple of setups/changes are required to the spreadsheet based on the spreadsheet version.

> Browser changes/configurations also need to be checked/enabled to access this new WEBADI layout/template in our machine

> New Integrator need to be developed for our requirement purpose, integrators are unique and we can't use them for other purpose, for example, I can't use the journal data template for the AP invoice uploading purpose.

> While creating integrator itself you are choosing interface name, interface type (API..etc) package and procedure..

> We also create next to the integrator, here we are determining the fields to be included in the layout.

> Then we will create the document with the required information, based on that only, when business user selected the document to be downloaded for the data entry, it will open as we designed

> Business user can enter/fill the data or he/she can copy the data from the other spreadsheet and can place it and then load it to the oracle application.

INVOICE AUTOMATION WITH MORE4APPS

Invoice creation in oracle payables can be done in two methods, one is with manual data entry and another one is through an interface. If we say an interface, it could be a third-party tool, custom program in oracle to support this requirement. Oracle can integrate with multiple software tools to automate the invoice processing, if we say automation, invoice entry. Invoice entry is the one of the essential for business organization.

We do have another best tool More4apps can easily automate the invoice processing in oracle applications. It will not be affect by the Patching/upgrade activity. More4apps is specifically designed for end-user to make the work easier, it will validate the data before we upload the data to the oracle application. It would be tested developed and tested by the more4apps support team, hence no need of any other testing needs to be done from our side.

Every functionality called as a Wizard in more4apps tool, AP Invoice is one Wizard and purchase order, customer, AR Receipts...Etc. are different wizards available in more4apps. These wizards are VBA program embedded in a Microsoft Excel workbook.

More4apps tool interfaces with the standard Oracle Open Interface table for AP invoices. It won't modify any other Oracle objects except during the installation, where it adds the More4Apps Batch Source in oracle.

Benefits of the More4apps integrations/automation with oracle apps.

➢ It will Creates any number of invoices and distributions, there is no limit..
➢ We can do matching for an invoice with a project or a purchase order
➢ We can downloads purchase order and receipt information to assist with matching
➢ Validates information before loading it into Oracle, processing messages are returned to the spreadsheet
➢ Just about any file format can be loaded into Excel, formatted, validated and loaded

All options are available on a ribbon format. Double-clicking in the spreadsheet also loads the forms. The forms are optional and you can simply type, import, or paste the values into the spreadsheet. We can upload Invoices one at a time, or your entire worksheet.

The program is flexible about the spreadsheet layout. We can move, delete, or hide unwanted columns. We can also have multiple sheets or even sheets in other workbooks. This program is supported on E-Business Suite for all the versions.

The AP Invoice worksheet separated into Invoice Header and Invoice Distribution sections. To enter an invoice you need a batch source selected and then enter the invoice header and distribution lines in the worksheet before uploading the invoices.

When installing the Wizard, Profile Options have been set up which enable us the below functionalities

➢ Allow a distribution in the worksheet to have no accounting source and still load into Oracle.

> ➢ Prevent the user from matching invoices to closed purchase orders.
> ➢ Override Function Security.
> ➢ Reject Zero values for Invoices.
> ➢ Suppress the matching of total invoice to total distributions.

By using this tool we can also update the existing invoice, normally oracle apps will strictly rejects to update the existing invoice, still by setting up a profile option in More4Apps, we can do the below activities

Cancel the existing Invoices in oracle – we have an ability to cancel the invoice in oracle apps by using this functionality from more4Apps. Update fields in Oracle for existing Invoices.

Normally there are two steps involved in the more4apps invoice load, one is validate and place the records in interface table and second one is importing the data to oracle base tables. Once the data is imported to oracle base tables, we can go and validate the data from the front end.

We had used this more4apps tool for our data migration for one of our prestigious client and it is very user-friendly and easy to work with spreadsheet.

We had used this tool for all our rollout projects for data migration and it is comfortable with oracle applications.

PAYMENT FILE AUTOMATION WITH APRO

The Oracle Payables module enables you to automate the invoice processing, implements business rules, systematizes routing and invoice approval, and leverages joint controls with other modules such as Financials and SCM and other products

It enables the reconciliation feature to make sure the vendor payments are done accurately…

Oracle payables will be integrating with many third-party tools. For example, payment-related banking gateways for the payment file generation and few tools for statement file importing and reconciliation.

Banking Gateways are fully transparent for the end-user, because it is possible to select the Oracle Payables Payment Batch by the Batch name or based on payment date. Payment batch name is nothing but a payment batch name which is entered by the business user during the payment run…also, the payment file data will be automatically transfer the payment data from oracle server to the PC automatically. This also can be taken care by the payment gateways…

There are multiple payment gateways which can be supported to do this activity. We have few tools as below.

1. Pay metric
2. APRO

Oracle Accounts Payable Payment file Generation

In this example, we will use APRO banking gateway in this example to explain how the payment file will get generated. By using Banking Gateway is impossible to do any updates in the Oracle Payables payment file. We can't change the vendor name and/or the vendor bank account number.

This is the one of the main reason to choose this automation of payment file generation and many of the clients will prefer to use it..

Bank statement file will be processed through APRO Banking payment Gateway to Oracle Financials product. In the APRO Banking Gateway, Invoice Number is identified by using the Invoice identification Rules of the APRO tool. Also, if Oracle Cash Management is used, it is possible based on the bank statement information to generate a bank transaction codes. These Transaction codes are used in Oracle Cash Management to generate automatically the posting to a General Ledger Account also to identify the receipt and payment.

The APRO Banking Gateway processes the data to the specified Open Interface of Oracle Financials. This means no technical interference is necessary to get this file from the PC to the Unix Server.

Out of Oracle Financials the created Payment file can be selected based on the batch name the end-user has specified. The payment batch is picked up from the Oracle Unix Server by the APRO Banking Gateway, next formatted to the Dutch file format ClieOp03, and put into the PC directory specified at the bank account number level in the APRO Banking Gateway.

Pictorial Representation:

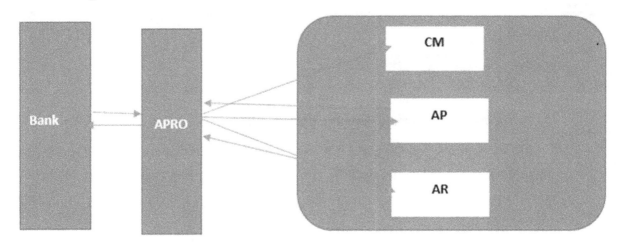

How Banking Gateway simplifies and automate the Oracle payments:

These payment gateways are supporting Oracle functionalities as below

➢ Addition of Customer Bank Account numbers automatically into Oracle receivables
➢ Customer Number Recognition based on Bank Account number
➢ Pay unrelated invoices , Use AutoCash Rule set as per the oracle setup, use Bank Transaction Codes to identify the payments and receipts
➢ Decide per bank account which Oracle Interface(s) must be used, f.e. CM or AR or CM and AR, but also GL only
➢ All data is stored in the Oracle Financials Database, as we have installed this tool on the oracle database, all data will be there in the oracle database and it won't
➢ Multiple Users can access this tool at the same time
➢ Can be managed central (or decentral)

➢ One product for all incoming and outgoing cash flows from/to Oracle Financials sold by one vendor. Save direct money and time

➢ All kind of bank statement records can be handled electronically, including direct debit rejections/reversals

➢ Audit trail of the bank statements and if requested the audit trail data can be exported to Excel or queried with use of a Business Intelligence Tool, for example Oracle Discoverer

➢ We have used this tool for Payment file generation and statement import in cash management to do the reconciliation

AUTOMATE YOUR PAYMENTS FROM ORACLE TO FINANCIAL INSTITUTION

The overall purpose of the blog is to import payments information from Payables module to Bank of America web bank interface. There is no need to apply conversion in as the report contains details of payment in payment currencies. We will be running this report/program multiple times bypassing the payment batch details as a parameter.

Normally business used to process the Payment batch and they will confirm the payment batch. After that business will take the payment file from the format instruction text output and placing the file in the bank interface or any other specified directory, so that from there bank used to take that file for the payment process. This is all the manual and lengthy process and not recommended as the manual intervention can make amendments to the payment file.

To avoid this manual intervention, one of our prestigious client has requested us to automate this process. so we have come up with a solution to automate the payment file movement to bank interface through a program. built a custom report called "XX BOA Payment OUTBOUND", which is in the prescribed format of BOA and a file is sent to the payment processor in a text format via email. BOA will take care of any duplicate payment files.

We do have "Final Payment register" in Oracle Payables is a default Report generated whenever a payment batch is confirmed. However, the default output of payment register is not in the prescribed format of BOA. Hence, we are developing a new "Final Payment Register"

➢ Business will generate a payment batch or create a quick payment for the Supplier Invoices.

➢ Business User will then submit final payment register after confirmation of the payment Batch.

➢ Payables will allow the user to generate this payment register as and when needed.

➢ User will upload the Payment register in text format data to BOA web bank interface as and when needed

➢ The import file validation for duplicity is the responsibility of the BOA.

➢ It is important to note that the date of payment batch date should be the date on which it is uploaded to BOA Web bank interface.

AMEX CREDIT CARD TRANSACTIONS

In oracle applications release 12 we have credit card functionality, which enabled in i-Expense. it allows users to select open credit card transactions and include them in user expense reports for claim processing. We have one of our prestigious client and they are running business around the globe. They have asked us to implement the credit card functionality, business has chosen, AMEX as the corporate credit card provider. Its have implemented this AMEX process to the client, we have used the below steps followed to implement this process.

➢ We need to check the card provider's file format in Internet Expenses, whether it will support or not

➢ It is always recommended that, one corporate card transactions file per each operating unit (except American Express GL1025 and GL1080 formats in Internet Expenses, the system requires one file per each operating unit that is defined in Oracle Financials and is implementing credit cards.)

➢ Determine payment liability (Individual Pay, Both Pay, Company Pay)

➢ We should have a file transfer virtuous connectivity

➢ We should be able to download the credit card transaction file by our self or we should be in a position to get the file to specified location.

The only pre-requisite for the organization would make an agreement with the credit card company to import an electronic file of credit card transactions that summarizes employees' expenses for a period. Once the electronic file is imported and validated, employees would be able to see their credit card transactions and then select them for expensing on their expense report.

When we planned to implement the corporate credit card functionality for Oracle Internet Expenses (OIE), we have 3 payment options available

a. Individual Pay
b. Both Pay
c. Company Pay

a. *Individual Pay*: Employee pays the credit card provider for all credit card transactions. Whether a user identifies credit card transactions as business or personal expenses, the user pays the credit card provider for all transactions. When the employee creates an expense report, only those transactions designated as business are reported on the expense report. The employee is eventually reimbursed by their employer for those credit card business expenses

b. *Both Pay*: The employee pays the credit card provider for personal expenses, and your company pays the credit card provider for business expenses. In this scenario, we have to make a payment directly to the credit card provider for the personal expenses by the user.

c. *Company Pay*: Company pays the credit card provider for all transactions, even though it is personal or the business transactions, company will make the payment to the credit card provider and will get the refund from the user.

To get the AMEX credit card transactions to the oracle, we need to follow the following steps.

These are the below file formats which are supported by the oracle internet expenses

➢ American Express KR1025 format
➢ American Express GL1025 format
➢ American Express GL1080 format

Below are the setups that are need to be configured based on the credit card provider, in that we have few setups which are mandatory

Step Number	Step	Required or Optional
1	Set up corporate card providers as suppliers	Required
2	Extend seeded card expense type lookup	Optional
3	Extend employee matching rules	Optional
4	Define source lookup for card expense type mapping rule	Optional
5	Define card expense type mapping rule	Optional
6	Set up expense clearing account	Optional
7	Set up credit card programs	Required
8	Set up credit card transaction file transfer parameters	Optional
9	Set up corporate card usage policies	Optional
10	Set up corporate card transaction submission policies	Optional
11	Set up card expense type mapping in expense template	Optional
12	Set up credit cards	Optional
13	Modify SQL Loader Scripts	Optional

Step Number	Step	Required or Optional
14	Modify credit card workflow processes	Optional
15	Use manage historical transaction management program to prepare for go-live	Optional
16	Enable credit card payment notifications	Optional
17	Enable credit card integration	Required

a. Setup Supplier and sup sites: Define the AMEX Credit card provider as a supplier, we must create the card providers and their payment addresses as suppliers and supplier sites in Oracle Payables. Payment terms and payment instrument must also be defined for each supplier and/or supplier site.

b. Extended CARD_EXPENSE_TYPE: it stores the credit card expense types that are used when a credit card transaction file is uploaded. The card expense types are used to map to the expense types defined in the expense template, this is a seeded look up and we can extend it based on the requirement.

c. Extended Employee Matching Rules: Internet Expenses enables our company to automatically create a new credit card when a transaction arrives for the card in the system for the first time. To enable the system to perform automatic card creation, we must assign an employee matching rule to the card program.

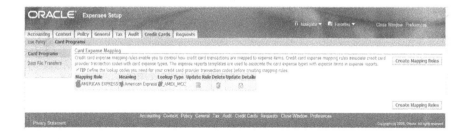

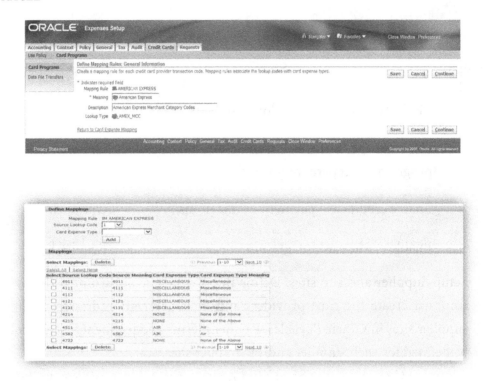

a. For AMEX master cards, we must define the Merchant Category Codes

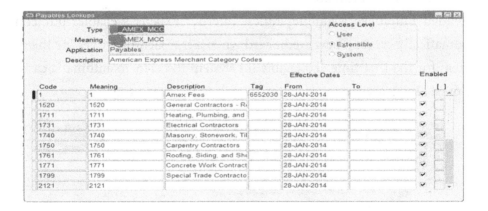

Once we have done all these required setups, we need to receive the statement file and then we need

"American Express Global Feed Transaction Loader and Validation Program"

```
-------------------------------------------------------------------------
ayables: Version : 12.1

opyright (c) 1998, 2013, Oracle and/or its affiliates. All rights reserved.

FKAAMEXGLTRX: American Express Global Feed Transaction Loader and Validation Program
-------------------------------------------------------------------------
urrent system time is 25-SEP-2019 16:45:14
-------------------------------------------------------------------------
rguments
---------------
GL_PROGRAM_NAME = AMERICAN EXPRESS
FILE_NAME = /interface/AP/data/inbound/AMEX/R554201_B000065612_GL1025_001
LOAD_PAYMENTS = Yes

ploading credit card transactions.
ep 25, 2019 4:46:30 PM oracle.adf.share.config.ADFConfigFactory findOrCreateADFConfig
NFO: oracle.adf.share.config.ADFConfigFactory No META-INF/adf-config.xml found
he file header is: 063612        554201    GL1025  0001 01 2019-09-25 19268 03 2007-08-21 P0 00000000000720 3402 +000000003954234 -000000000579265 070612000
he file trailer is: 963612       554201    GL1025  0001 01 2019-09-25 19268 03 2007-09-21 P0 00000000000720 3402 +000000003954234 -000000000579265 070612000
78 credit card transactions were successfully uploaded.
umber of new credit card accounts registered: 1.

alidating 478 transactions.
ows valid: 478.
-------------------------------------------------------------------------
tart of log messages from FND_FILE
-------------------------------------------------------------------------
-------------------------------------------------------------------------
```

VISA CREDIT CARD TRANSACTIONS

In oracle applications release 12 we have credit card functionality, which enabled in i-Expense. it allows users to select open credit card transactions and include them in user expense reports for claim processing.

Internet Expenses currently supports the credit card functionality and here in this chapter I would like you to go through the process of VISA credit card integration with the oracle application. Currently oracle applications supports the following file formats.

➢ Visa VCF3 format
➢ Visa VCF4 format
➢ Bank of America Visa TS2 format
➢ US Bank Visa format

We need to perform the couple of basic setups which we have already discussed in our previous topic AMEX statement interface to oracle application. Hence we are discussing the process for the VISA cards.

Process a Company Pay expense report:

1. On a daily basis, obtain the credit card transactions data file from our credit card provider.
2. Load and validate your transactions. *"Visa VCF 4 Transaction Loader and Validation Program"*

```
+--------------------------------------------------------------+
Payables: Version : 12.1

Copyright (c) 1998, 2013, Oracle and/or its affiliates. All rights reserved.

APXVVCF4: Visa VCF 4 Transaction Loader and Validation Program
+--------------------------------------------------------------+
Current system time is 05-NOV-2019 22:06:09

+--------------------------------------------------------------+
Arguments
------------------------
P_CARD_PROGRAM_ID = 10020
P_FILE_NAME = /interface/AP/data/inbound/WELLSFARGO/1_6369
------------------------

Uploading credit card transactions.
Nov 06, 2019 10:06:24 PM oracle.adf.share.config.ADFConfigFactory findOrCreateADFConfig
INFO: oracle.adf.share.config.ADFConfigFactory No META-INF/adf-config.xml found
10 credit card transactions were successfully uploaded.

Validating 8 transactions.
Rows failed due to an inactive card number: 3.
Rows valid: 5.
Rows invalid: 3.
+--------------------------------------------------------------+
Start of log messages from FND_FILE
+--------------------------------------------------------------+
+--------------------------------------------------------------+
End of log messages from FND_FILE
+--------------------------------------------------------------+
```

3. Create and import the credit card provider invoice.

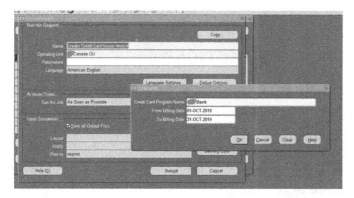

To create the credit card provider invoice and import it into Oracle Payables, you must run the Create Credit Card Issuer Invoice program in Payables. This will be scheduled to run on a daily basis.

Responsibility: AP Super User

Credit Card providerInvoice: 3062749-01-FEB-18

In this example, there are expenses for 2 employees:

Shannon Tremblay =   590.91

Kenn Richards =   922.80

Total = 1,513.71

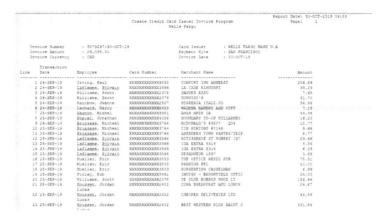

Credit Card provider Invoice: 3067743-17-FEB-18

In this example, there are expenses for one employee

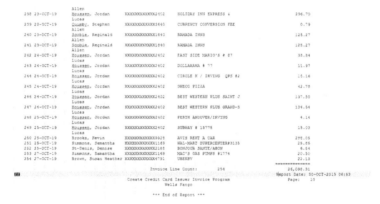

After the import, the AP header record appears as follows:

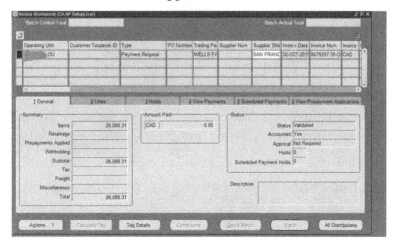

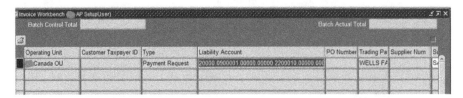

And the distribution appears as follows. All lines of the file are charged to the "default clearing account". The default has been defined as 20000-0900001-00000-00000-2200020.

The Accounting entry created by loading the daily transactions is:

DR Clearing Account - 20000.0900001.00000.00000.2200020.00000.0000.0000.0000

CR Trade AP (to xxxxxxx) 20000.0900001.00000.00000.2200010.00000.0000.0000.0000

This entry is created at the summary level per employee.

   a. Employee creates and submits expense report.
   b. After the file is loaded in Step 2 below, the transactions are matched to employee records in iExpense and employees can complete expense reports.

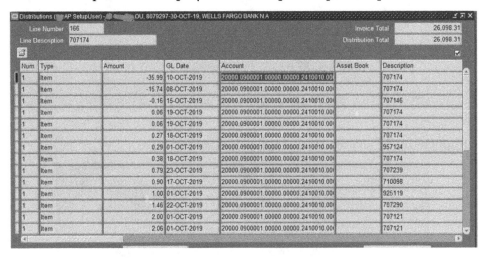

   c. Submission of employee expense reports will work the same as Amex charges in the previous topic. When users create expense reports, they select the credit card transactions that they want to submit on an expense report. During this step, users determine if transactions are business or personal expenses. Users will be reimbursed by their employers for only cash and other business expenses. (Cash and other expenses represent expenses that were not charged to the company credit card but are business expenses.) They will not be reimbursed for any business credit card expenses.

d. Credit card transactions designated as personal expenses will reduce the amount that the employee will be reimbursed. Once processed on an expense report, credit card transactions are no longer available in the list of transactions to be added to expense reports. This is true for both business and personal expenses.

AUTOMATE EXPENSE ALLOCATION

Multi-period accounting enables users to create accounting for a single accounting event for more than one GL period. The functionality is primarily used to recognize our prepaid expense across multiple GL Periods. We do have automated recognition of prepaid expenses, here in this blog we will discuss on the prepaid expenses, how do we allocate to the multiple periods.

Multi-Period Accounting, it's a feature available in R12 to accrue an amount and then prorate the same as expense across future periods. For more details on MPA, please refer White paper on Multi-Period Accounting (Note 1315106.1). Organization receives payable invoice for Insurance premium. The invoice is for insurance for next one year. As per accounting principle "Expense to be recognized as and when services are rendered", following should happen as far as Accounting of the Insurance invoice is concerned:

a. Expense of Insurance Invoice should not be recognized the day invoice is recorded. This need to be done as insurance service is yet NOT delivered the day respective invoice is recorded.

b. Insurance service is going to be rendered over a period of coming Year, hence the insurance expense should be recorded in future accounting periods as and when it comes.

Setups required for MPA

a. We need to have the required accounts, insurance Expense account and Insurance prepayment a/c
b. We need to define invoice line flex field
c. We need ADR (Accounting derivation rule change)
d. Journal line type need to be defined
e. Assign MPA Journal Line Types to Journal Line Definitions (JLD)
f. Assign JLD to Application Accounting Definition (AAD)
g. Assign AAD to sub-ledger accounting method

INVOICE CANCELLATION API

We need or want to cancel an invoice, Oracle Payables allows us to cancel only unpaid invoices. In addition these invoices cannot be on holds, have applied prepayments, or have been matched to a permanently closed PO. If the invoices are having any prepayments, we cannot cancel the prepayments if they are applied to the invoices. If the invoices are placed on postable hold, these invoices must be released from the holds prior to being cancelled. If we cancel an invoice, we will no longer be able to make changes to it. To cancel invoice distributions, we must reverse them. When Oracle Payables cancels an invoice, it sets the invoice amount and all its scheduled payments to zero. It also reverses the invoice distributions of the invoice and any PO matches. It also submits invoice approval, and if there are no postable holds.

If we want to cancel an invoice, we use the invoice Workbench. Enter the selection criteria and click on the Find button to locate the invoice you want to cancel. From the invoices form, select the action button. The invoice actions form will appear. To cancel invoice, check the Cancel Invoices checkbox and click on OK. The invoice will be cancelled if there are no postable holds

AP_CANCEL_PKG.IS_INVOICE_CANCELLABLE

Is_Invoice_Cancellable is a Function in the AP_CANCEL_PKG package that checks that an Invoice is cancellable or not when an Invoice Cancellation process starts. It follows the following steps and returns a Boolean value depending on the result.

AP invoice contains distribution that does not have open GL period return FALSE.

- ➢ Invoice has an effective payment, return FALSE.
- ➢ If the invoice is in selected for payment status, return FALSE.
- ➢ Invoice was already cancelled and we are using the API to cancel.
- ➢ If invoice is credited invoice, return FALSE.
- ➢ If invoices have been applied against this invoice, return FALSE.
- ➢ If invoice is matched to Finally Closed PO's, return FALSE.
- ➢ If project-related invoices have pending adjustments, return FALSE.
- ➢ If cancelling will cause qty_billed or amount_billed to less than 0, return FALSE.
- ➢ If none of above, invoice is cancellable return True.

Here is a small procedure to check if an Invoice is cancellable or not.

```
CREATE OR REPLACE PROCEDURE xx_inv_cancellable (p_inv_id IN NUMBER)
IS
   v_boolean        BOOLEAN;
   v_error_code     VARCHAR2 (100);
   v_debug_info     VARCHAR2 (1000);
BEGIN
   v_boolean :=
      ap_cancel_pkg.is_invoice_cancellable (p_invoice_id          => p_inv_id,
                                            p_error_code                    =>
v_error_code,
                                            p_debug_info                    =>
v_debug_info,
                                            p_calling_sequence    => NULL
                                            );
   IF v_boolean = TRUE
   THEN
      DBMS_OUTPUT.put_line ('Invoice ' || p_inv_id || ' is cancellable');
   ELSE
```

```
        DBMS_OUTPUT.put_line (    'Invoice '
                              || p_inv_id
                              || ' is not cancellable :'
                              || v_error_code
                          );
    END IF;
END xx_inv_cancellable;
EXECUTE XX_INV_CANCELLABLE(12960);
```

AP_CANCEL_PKG.AP_CANCEL_SINGLE_INVOICE

AP_CANCEL_SINGLE_INVOICE is a Function in the AP_CANCEL_PKG package that cancels one invoice by executing the following sequence of steps, returning TRUE if successful and FALSE otherwise.

- ➢ Check if the invoice is cancellable. If yes, precede otherwise return false
- ➢ If invoice has tax withheld, undo withholding
- ➢ Clear out all payment schedules
- ➢ Cancel all the non-discard lines
- ➢ Reverse matching
- ➢ Fetch the maximum distribution line number
- ➢ Set encumbered flags to 'N'
- ➢ Accounting event generation
- ➢ Reverse the distributions
- ➢ Update Line level Cancelled information
- ➢ Zero out the Invoice
- ➢ Run Auto Approval for this invoice
- ➢ Check posting holds remain on this cancelled invoice
- ➢ If NOT exist – complete the cancellation by updating header level information set return value to TRUE
- ➢ If exist – no update, set the return values to FALSE, NO DATA rollback. Commit the Data
- ➢ Populate the out parameters

Here is a small procedure to cancel a single invoice.

```
CREATE OR REPLACE PROCEDURE xx_inv_cancel (
    p_xx_invoice_id        IN  NUMBER,
    p_xx_last_updated_by   IN  NUMBER,
    p_xx_last_update_login IN  NUMBER,
    p_xx_accounting_date   IN  DATE
)
IS
    v_boolean              BOOLEAN;
    v_message_name         VARCHAR2 (1000);
    v_invoice_amount       NUMBER;
    v_base_amount          NUMBER;
    v_temp_cancelled_amount NUMBER;
    v_cancelled_by         VARCHAR2 (1000);
    v_cancelled_amount     NUMBER;
    v_cancelled_date       DATE;
    v_last_update_date     DATE;
    v_orig_prepay_amt      NUMBER;
    v_pay_cur_inv_amt      NUMBER;
    v_token                VARCHAR2 (100);
BEGIN
    v_boolean :=
      ap_cancel_pkg.ap_cancel_single_invoice
              (p_invoice_id              => p_xx_invoice_id,
               p_last_updated_by         => p_xx_last_updated_by,
               p_last_update_login       => p_xx_last_update_login,
               p_accounting_date         => p_xx_accounting_date,
               p_message_name            => v_message_name,
               p_invoice_amount          => v_invoice_amount,
               p_base_amount             => v_base_amount,
               p_temp_cancelled_amount   => v_temp_cancelled_amount,
               p_cancelled_by            => v_cancelled_by,
               p_cancelled_amount        => v_cancelled_amount,
               p_cancelled_date          => v_cancelled_date,
               p_last_update_date        => v_last_update_date,

               p_original_prepayment_amount => v_orig_prepay_amt,
               p_pay_cur_invoice_amount     => v_pay_cur_inv_amt,
               p_token                   => v_token,
               p_calling_sequence        => NULL
              );

    IF v_boolean
    THEN
       DBMS_OUTPUT.put_line ('Successfully Cancelled the Invoice');
       COMMIT;
    ELSE
       DBMS_OUTPUT.put_line ('Failed to Cancel the Invoice');
       ROLLBACK;
    END IF;
END xx_inv_cancel;

EXECUTE XX_INV_CANCEL(120573,2325,-1,SYSDATE);
```

ALERTS TO AUTOMATE OUR ANALYSIS

In Oracle Application, we do have a fantastic functionality Alert. We can control our database by knowing some important or unexpected activity in the database. Alerts can ensure that, you are regularly and quickly informed about critical database events instead of sorting through length reports.

There are two types of alerts available in oracle applications.

a. Event Alert
b. Periodical Alert

Event Alert: If we have chosen event alert, it will immediately notifies us, when any activity happens on our database as it occurs. These Alerts are fired/triggered based on some change in data in the database/tables. Ex: If you want to notify your team on any of the table column populated with status as Error, we can use Event-based alerts. When we create any expense reports from oracle internet expenses, it will create a new record and add the status to the ap_expense_report_headers_all in the column expense_status_code, here inserting a record in the table is an event so whenever a new record is inserted it will send the alert. In same alert you can also send the information to the one person or the team

Periodic Alerts: These periodic Alerts can be triggered hourly, daily, weekly, monthly and yearly based on our requirement/configuration. If we want to know list of all errors on the AP_EXPENSE_REPORT_HEADERS_ALL table, created on that day at the end of the day we can use periodic alerts. This alert will notify you every day regardless of data entered or not on that day. Even if we did not create any new expense reports on that day but if some data exists on the table with errors. It will send the alert to the required person/team for taking corrective action.

We had a requirement from the business as below, One of our prestigious client is used to operate the business across the globe and they have implemented oracle internet expenses module for claim process. They have reported that, business could submit expense reports and they are going on error and business end-user sometimes not aware of it and waiting for the refund. Later they are realizing and reaching out to IT Support team.. to avoid this we have come up with an automation process to check all these errors mechanically, ie: Alerts . we have a defined a periodic alert which can trigger the notification to the IT Support along with all the error details" also, we had included a SQL query to fetch all the employee, user, supervisor, code combinations, expense items..etc so it will made the analysis very easy to identify the issue to fix it.

Please find the below steps to define the Alerts

Navigate to Alert Manager>>Alert>>Define

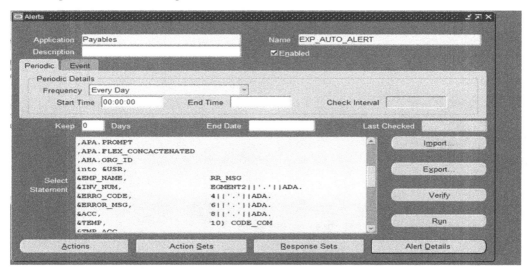

We have used the below query to get the alert to be triggered with all the required details..

Please find the sample script for your reference.

```
select FU.USER_NAME,
PAP.FULL_NAME ,
AHA.INVOICE_NUM,
AHA.EXPENSE_STATUS_CODE
,ALA.AP_VALIDATION_ERROR ERR_MSG
,(ADA.SEGMENT1||'.'||ADA.SEGMENT2||'.'||ADA.SEGMENT3||'.'||ADA.SEGMENT4||
'.'||ADA.SEGMENT5||'.'||ADA.SEGMENT6||'.'||ADA.SEGMENT7||'.'||ADA.SEGMENT
8||'.'||ADA.SEGMENT9||'.'||ADA.SEGMENT10) CODE_COM
,APA.PROMPT
,APA.FLEX_CONCACTENATED
,AHA.ORG_ID
into &USR,
```

```
&EMP_NAME,
&INV_NUM,
&ERRO_CODE,
&ERROR_MSG,
&ACC,
&TEMP,
&TMP_ACC,
&ORG
from APPS.AP_EXP_REPORT_DISTS_ALL ADA
,APPS.AP_EXPENSE_REPORT_HEADERS_ALL AHA
,APPS.AP_EXPENSE_REPORT_LINES_ALL ALA
,apps.AP_EXPENSE_REPORT_PARAMS_ALL apa
,APPS.FND_USER FU
,APPS.PER_ALL_PEOPLE_F PAP
where 1=1
and FU.EMPLOYEE_ID=AHA.EMPLOYEE_ID
and ADA.REPORT_LINE_ID(+)=ALA.REPORT_LINE_ID
and PAP.PERSON_ID=AHA.EMPLOYEE_ID
and aha.expense_report_id=apa.expense_report_id
and AHA.REPORT_HEADER_ID=ALA.REPORT_HEADER_ID
--and AHA.EXPENSE_STATUS_CODE = 'ERROR'
and APA.PARAMETER_ID=ALA.WEB_PARAMETER_ID
and INVOICE_NUM='Web355020'
and APA.ORG_ID=AHA.ORG_ID
```

AUTOMATE YOUR INTERFACE CLEANING

As the present trend is to reduce the manual involvement or to allow human errors is not an suggestable activity for the larger-scale industries. As the organization grows, the data will also become huge volume and we need to make sure to delete the Stage/interface tables to XXprove the performance. In this example, we will discuss how we had automated the sales orders interface clearing frequently.

We need to follow the below steps to achieve the same.

a. Create Value sets.

   Application Developer→Validation→Set

   Value Set Name: XX_INV_ORG

   Description: XX Inventory Org From The Stagging Table

   List Type:List of Values

   Format Type:Char

   MaxXXum Size:30

   Validation Type:Table

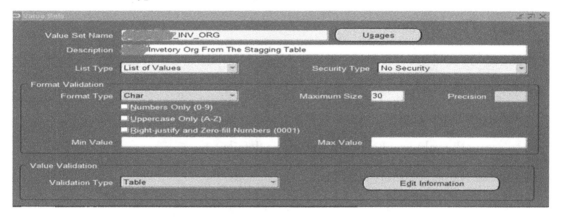

   Click On Edit Information

   Table Application: client Custom

   Table Name: (SELECT DISTINCT INVENTORY_ORG FROM XXX_SALESORDERS_STG) A

   Value: INVENTORY_ORG

   Type: Char

   Size: 30

a. Value Set Name: XXX_CUSTOMER_NUM

   Description: XXX Customer Number From The Stagging Table

   List Type: List of Values

   Format Type: Char

   MaxXXum Size: 30

   Validation Type: Table

We need to create the value set based on the above details.

   Value Set Name: XX_SO _STATUS

   Description: XX SO status From The Stagging Table

   List Type: List of Values

   Format Type: Char

   MaxXXum Size: 30

   Validation Type: Table

We need to define the value set with the following information, This value set is used for status parameter, in which state the stage record is in...

a. Register as a concurrent program
   Application Developer → Concurrent→Program

   Program: XX Sales Order Interface Delete

   Short Name: XX_SO_INT_DELETE

Application: Client Custom

Description: XXX Sales Order Interface Delete

Executable Name: XXX_SO_INT_DELETE_SN

Method: PL/SQL Stored Procedure

Once we have register this program, either this can be schedule or on-demand we can run to clear the interface records which are in stage and causing issues while processing sales orders. Still we feel there is a gap and manual work is required and what we had done is, we have included this in the original program. We have an integration for sales orders creation program, for that only we have created this stage table clearing program. We had amended the original program by writing a shell script which will automatically call this child job when the original request is errored because of any data issues, system will automatically deletes/purge the data from the stage tables automatically. By doing this business was very much happy as they no need to reach out to IT for stage clearing as and if you don't clear the stage and re-tried to process the file, it will get failed as the orphan data available in the stage tables. it will also XXproves the application performance.

Output Format:

```
      Sales Orders Cleared From The Staging Table By Following Parameters
INVENTORY ORG:
CUSTOMER NUMBER:99131.00123
STATUS:U
No Of Records Deleted:1
SALES AGREEMENT NUMBER|SALES AGREEMENT TYPE|CUSTOMER NUMBER|INVENTORY ORG|ORDER PERIOD|ORDER_ITEM|PRICE|ORDER QUANTITY|STATUS|ERROR CODE|ERROR MESSAGE|CREATED BY|LAST
||99131.00123|INSIGHT|19-JUN|INS-PS-1|9000|1|U|||AUTOINSTALL|
```

```
CREATE OR REPLACE PROCEDURE APPS.XX_XXDC_SO_INT_DELETE_PROC(P_ERRBUF OUT
VARCHAR2

                                                    , P_RETCODE
OUT NUMBER

                                                    , P_INV_ORG
VARCHAR2

                                                    , P_CUST_NUM
VARCHAR2

                                                    , P_STATUS
```

```
VARCHAR2)

                                                    --
,P_SO_AGRMNT_TYPE VARCHAR2

                                                    --
,P_SO_AGRMNT_NUM  VARCHAR2)
AS
V_COUNT NUMBER;
 CURSOR xx_SO IS

     SELECT IIS.SALES_AGREEMENT_NUMBER

           ,IIS.SALES_AGREEMENT_TYPE

           ,IIS.CUSTOMER_NUMBER

           ,IIS.INVENTORY_ORG

           ,IIS.ORDER_PERIOD

           ,IIS.ORDER_ITEM

           ,IIS.PRICE

           ,IIS.ORDER_QUANTITY

           ,IIS.STATUS

           ,IIS.ERROR_CODE

           ,IIS.ERROR_MESSAGE

           ,(SELECT DISTINCT USER_NAME

               FROM FND_USER FU

             WHERE 1=1

               AND FU.USER_ID=IIS.CREATED_BY)      CREATED_BY

           ,(SELECT DISTINCT USER_NAME

               FROM FND_USER FU
```

```
                WHERE 1=1

                    AND FU.USER_ID=IIS.LAST_UPDATED_BY) LAST_UPDATAED_BY

        FROM xx_XXDCORDERS_STG IIS

       WHERE 1=1

        AND IIS.INVENTORY_ORG            =  NVL(P_INV_ORG,IIS.INVENTORY_ORG)

        AND IIS.CUSTOMER_NUMBER          =
NVL(P_CUST_NUM,IIS.CUSTOMER_NUMBER)

        AND IIS.STATUS                   =  NVL(P_STATUS,IIS.STATUS);
   --     AND NVL(IIS.SALES_AGREEMENT_TYPE,'Y')    =
NVL(NVL(P_SO_AGRMNT_TYPE,IIS.SALES_AGREEMENT_TYPE),'Y')
   --     AND NVL(IIS.SALES_AGREEMENT_NUMBER,1)=
NVL(NVL(P_SO_AGRMNT_NUM,IIS.SALES_AGREEMENT_NUMBER),1);

 BEGIN


   SELECT COUNT(*) INTO V_COUNT

     FROM xx_XXDCORDERS_STG IIS

      WHERE 1=1

        AND IIS.INVENTORY_ORG           =  NVL(P_INV_ORG,IIS.INVENTORY_ORG)

        AND IIS.CUSTOMER_NUMBER         =
NVL(P_CUST_NUM,IIS.CUSTOMER_NUMBER)

        AND IIS.STATUS                  =  NVL(P_STATUS,IIS.STATUS);


      IF V_COUNT='0' THEN


FND_FILE.PUT_LINE(FND_FILE.OUTPUT,'*****************************************
No Records Found in Staging to
```

```
Delete******************************************'

  );

 ELSE

   FND_FILE.PUT_LINE(FND_FILE.OUTPUT, 'XXDC Sales Orders Cleared From The
Staging Table By Following Parameters'
);

   FND_FILE.PUT_LINE(FND_FILE.OUTPUT,  'INVENTORY ORG:'
||P_INV_ORG     );

     FND_FILE.PUT_LINE(FND_FILE.OUTPUT,'CUSTOMER NUMBER:'
||P_CUST_NUM                               );

   FND_FILE.PUT_LINE(FND_FILE.OUTPUT,'STATUS:'
||P_STATUS                 );

     FND_FILE.PUT_LINE(FND_FILE.OUTPUT,'No Of Records Deleted:'
||V_COUNT       );


FND_FILE.PUT_LINE(FND_FILE.OUTPUT,'SALES AGREEMENT NUMBER'

                               ||'|'||     'SALES AGREEMENT TYPE'

                               ||'|'|| 'CUSTOMER NUMBER'

                               ||'|'||'INVENTORY ORG'

                               ||'|'||'ORDER PERIOD'

                               ||'|'||'ORDER_ITEM'

                               ||'|'||'PRICE'

                               ||'|'||'ORDER QUANTITY'

                               ||'|'|| 'STATUS'

                               ||'|'||'ERROR CODE'

                               ||'|'||  'ERROR MESSAGE'
```

126

```
                                      ||'|'|||'CREATED BY'

                                      ||'|'|||'LAST UPDATED BY');

FOR XX IN XX_SO

LOOP

FND_FILE.PUT_LINE(FND_FILE.OUTPUT,XX.SALES_AGREEMENT_NUMBER

                              ||'|'|||XX.SALES_AGREEMENT_TYPE

                              ||'|'|||XX.CUSTOMER_NUMBER

                              ||'|'|||XX.INVENTORY_ORG

                              ||'|'|||XX.ORDER_PERIOD

                              ||'|'|||XX.ORDER_ITEM

                              ||'|'|||XX.PRICE

                              ||'|'|||XX.ORDER_QUANTITY

                              ||'|'|||XX.STATUS

                              ||'|'|||XX.ERROR_CODE

                              ||'|'|||XX.ERROR_MESSAGE

                              ||'|'|||XX.CREATED_BY

                              ||'|'|||XX.LAST_UPDATAED_BY);

END LOOP;


BEGIN

DELETE FROM XX_XXDCORDERS_STG IIS

WHERE 1=1

    AND IIS.INVENTORY_ORG          =   NVL(P_INV_ORG,IIS.INVENTORY_ORG)

    AND IIS.CUSTOMER_NUMBER        =   NVL(P_CUST_NUM,IIS.CUSTOMER_NUMBER)

    AND IIS.STATUS                 =   NVL(P_STATUS,IIS.STATUS);
```

```
-- AND NVL(IIS.SALES_AGREEMENT_TYPE,'Y')    =
NVL(NVL(P_SO_AGRMNT_TYPE,IIS.SALES_AGREEMENT_TYPE),'Y')

-- AND NVL(IIS.SALES_AGREEMENT_NUMBER,1)=
NVL(NVL(P_SO_AGRMNT_NUM,IIS.SALES_AGREEMENT_NUMBER),1);

COMMIT;

END;

END IF;

EXCEPTION

WHEN OTHERS THEN

NULL;

END;

/
```

A SIMPLIFY YOUR RECONCILIATION BETWEEN GL AND SUB LEDGERS (AP & AR, CM)

During Month End time, reconciliation is an important activity between GL and other sub-ledgers are highly recommended. If AP balance interfaced to GL, verifying the balance between the two applications usually done through comparing account balances of the liability (A/P Trading) account. If we take AR as a sub-ledger we are going to verify the receivable account balance between the GL and AR.

If we want to do the reconciliation, we have to run couple of reports to make sure that the balance has been matched or not. If not matching then we need to run other couple of reports to identify the issue.

If we take AP reconciliation is an example, Compare the ending accounts payable account balance in the general ledger for the immediately preceding period to the aged accounts payable detail report as of the end of the same period. If these numbers do not match, you will have to reconcile earlier periods before attempting to reconcile the current period. If the variance is immaterial, it may be acceptable to proceed with the reconciliation for the current period.

We need to make sure the balance is correct from the AP side. Means current month AP TB balance is accurate or any issues. to make sure that we have to run the below reports manually.

a. Accounts Payables Trial balance for the previous month
b. Payables posted invoice register for the current month
c. Payables posted payments register for the current month
d. Accounts Payables Trial balance for the current month

We need to follow the below formula to calculate the current month AP TB balance.

Prev AP TB close Bal + current Month Inv register Bal – current month Payment register bal = Current month AP TB BAL.

We need to take the GL trail balance for that period and need to match with the AP TB balance with GL balance for the liability account.

Note: All these process is MANUAL Work

Also if we take AR to GL Reconciliation, we need to run couple reports to make sure the AR balance is correct. Means, need to make sure aging 7 buckets (outstanding report) is showing correct balance, before we do the reconciliation. To make sure that we have to run the below reports.

a. Aging 7 buckets for Prev Month
b. Transaction Register
c. Invoice Exceptions
d. Applied Receipts
e. Unapplied receipts
f. Adjustments
g. Aging 7 buckets for the current month

All these reports need to be run manually and due to system performance it may take longer time or it will be consuming huge man-hours for reconciliation. To overcome this situation we have come up with a solution as a single report, which will automatically shows all these reconciliation details and variations.

Actually we do have a standard report "Account analysis Report" which will be used to extract the data based on the source. By extending this report we had achieved this solution

Functionality of the Standard report is to review source, category and reference information to trace our functional currency or STAT transactions back to their original source. You can run this report with entry, line or source item reference information to help identify the origin of journals created by Journal Import. This report prints the journal entry lines and beginning and ending balances of the accounts you request. For each journal entry line, the report prints the source, category, batch name, journal entry name, account, description, entry/line/source item reference information, and the debit or credit amount.

Custom report: The standard Report is displaying batch-wise details based on account number per particular period (debits and credits). In one batch it may include different transactions. Here in our business case we want to know summary data based on source name

- o The Report output should be in Excel Format.
- o If source of Data from payables means Report should display supplier details like Supplier name, Supplier number, Invoice amount, Invoice Date, GL Date.(it include open invoices, paid and Partial paid, Prepaid invoices)
- o If source of data from Receivables means Report should display customer details like customer Name, Customer Number, Invoice Amount, Invoice Date, GL date. If receipt is created for invoice then should display receipt details in the place of invoice details.
- o Reconciliation With GL Trail balance Report. Account Analysis debit amount, credit Amount, Beginning Balance, ending Balance must be match with 'GL Trail balance Report

Debit amount, credit Amount, Beginning Balance, ending Balance for the Particular account.

Output

Sample report

```
SAMPLE query-----------------------------------------------------------------
-----------------------------------

SELECT distinct XAH.ACCOUNTING_DATE
GL_DATE ,

      RCTA.TRX_DATE
INVOICE_DATE,

      XAL.CODE_COMBINATION_ID,

      RCTTA.NAME
TRANSACTION_TYPE,

      NVL(RCTA.INTERFACE_HEADER_ATTRIBUTE2, RCTA.ATTRIBUTE2)
SRH,

      RCTA.TRX_NUMBER
INVOICE_NUMBER,

      Hp.Party_Name
Customer_Name,

      RCTTA.DESCRIPTION,

     (SELECT concatenated_segments

      FROM GL_CODE_COMBINATIONS_KFV  GCCKFV

      WHERE XAL.ACCOUNTED_DR IS NOT NULL

      AND GCCKFV.CODE_COMBINATION_ID=XAL.CODE_COMBINATION_ID)
DR_ACCOUNT,

     (SELECT CONCATENATED_SEGMENTS

      FROM GL_CODE_COMBINATIONS_KFV GCCKFV

      WHERE XAL.ACCOUNTED_CR IS NOT NULL

      AND GCCKFV.CODE_COMBINATION_ID=XAL.CODE_COMBINATION_ID)
CR_ACCOUNT,
```

```
        xal.accounting_class_code,

        Apsa.Amount_Due_Original
INVOICE_TOTAL

FROM    Ra_Customer_Trx_All              Rcta,

        Ra_Cust_Trx_Types_All            Rctta,

        Ar_Payment_Schedules_All         Apsa,

        Hz_Parties                       Hp,

        Hz_Cust_Accounts_All             Hcaa,

        Xla.Xla_Ae_Headers               Xah,

        Xla.Xla_Ae_Lines                 Xal,

        Xla.Xla_Events                   Xe,

        Xla.Xla_Transaction_Entities     Xte,

        Gl_Import_References             Gir,

        Gl_Je_Batches                    Gjb,

        Gl_Je_Headers                    Gjh,

        Gl_Je_Lines                      Gjl

        -- Xle_Entity_Profiles          Xep
Where Hp.Party_Id            = Hcaa.Party_Id

And   Hcaa.Cust_Account_Id   = Rcta.Bill_To_Customer_Id

And   Rctta.Cust_Trx_Type_Id = Rcta.Cust_Trx_Type_Id

And   Rcta.Customer_Trx_Id   = Xte.Source_Id_Int_1

And   Xah.Ae_Header_Id       = Xal.Ae_Header_Id

And   Xal.Ledger_Id          = Xte.Ledger_Id

And   Xah.Application_Id      = Xal.Application_Id

And   Xe.Event_Id            = Xah.Event_Id

And   Xe.Entity_Id           = Xte.Entity_Id
```

```
And    Gir.Gl_Sl_Link_Id          = Xal.Gl_Sl_Link_Id

AND    Gir.Gl_Sl_Link_Table       = Xal.Gl_Sl_Link_Table

--AND   GJh.je_source              = 'Receivables'

And    Gir.Je_Batch_Id            = Gjb.Je_Batch_Id

And    Gir.Je_Header_Id           = Gjh.Je_Header_Id

And    Gjh.Ledger_Id              = Xah.Ledger_Id

And    Gjh.Je_Header_Id           = Gjl.Je_Header_Id

AND    Xal.Code_Combination_Id    = Gjl.Code_Combination_Id

AND    RCTa.TRX_NUMBER='10047'-----------10047----10048

AND    Rcta.Customer_Trx_Id       = Apsa.Customer_Trx_Id

AND    RCTA.TRX_NUMBER            = XTE.TRANSACTION_NUMBER

--AND   RCTTA.NAME                 =:P_TRANSACTION_TYPE

--AND   TRUNC(XAL.ACCOUNTING_DATE) BETWEEN
NVL(:P_FROM_GL_DATE,TRUNC(XAL.ACCOUNTING_DATE)) AND
NVL(:P_TO_GL_DATE,TRUNC(XAL.ACCOUNTING_DATE));
```



```
select AIA.gl_date,

       APS.VENDOR_NAME,

       APS.SEGMENT1  SUPPLIER_NO,

       XDL.EVENT_CLASS_CODE EVENT_CLASS,

       AIA.INVOICE_ID,

       AID.INVOICE_DISTRIBUTION_ID,
```

```
        AIA.INVOICE_NUM   TRANSACTION_NUMBER,

        AIA.INVOICE_DATE,

        INITCAP(GJL.DESCRIPTION) DESCRIPTION,

        GJH.JE_HEADER_ID,

        XDL.AE_HEADER_ID,

        XDL.AE_LINE_NUM,

        XTE.SOURCE_ID_INT_1,

        XTE.APPLICATION_ID,

        XTE.ENTITY_ID,

        GJH.JE_SOURCE,

        GJH.JE_CATEGORY,

        XEP.name
LEGAL_ENTITY_NAME ,

        (SELECT concatenated_segments

        FROM GL_CODE_COMBINATIONS_KFV  GCCKFV

        where XAL.ACCOUNTED_DR is not null

        AND GCCKFV.CODE_COMBINATION_ID=XAL.CODE_COMBINATION_ID)
DR_ACCOUNT_CS,

        (SELECT CONCATENATED_SEGMENTS

        FROM GL_CODE_COMBINATIONS_KFV GCCKFV

        where XAL.ACCOUNTED_CR is not null

        and GCCKFV.CODE_COMBINATION_ID=XAL.CODE_COMBINATION_ID)
CR_ACCOUNT_CS,

        XAL.ACCOUNTING_CLASS_CODE,

        GJL.ACCOUNTED_DR                                    DEBIT,

        GJL.ACCOUNTED_CR                                    CREDIT,

        AIA.INVOICE_AMOUNT,
```

```
      AIA.AMOUNT_PAID,

      AIA.PAYMENT_STATUS_FLAG

    ---   (Nvl(GJl.Accounted_Dr, 0))-(Nvl(GJl.Accounted_Cr, 0)) Net_Amount

from

      Xla.Xla_Ae_Headers              Xah,

      Xla.Xla_Ae_Lines               Xal,

      Xla.Xla_Events                 Xe,

      Xla.Xla_Transaction_Entities    Xte,

      Gl_Import_References           Gir,

      Gl_Je_Batches                  Gjb,

      GL_JE_HEADERS                  GJH,

      GL_JE_LINES                    GJL,

      XLE_ENTITY_PROFILES            XEP,

      XLA_DISTRIBUTION_LINKS         XDL,

      AP_INVOICES_ALL                AIA,

      AP_INVOICE_DISTRIBUTIONS_ALL    AID,

      ap_suppliers                   aps

where 1=1

and   XAH.AE_HEADER_ID              = XAL.AE_HEADER_ID

and   XAL.LEDGER_ID                 = XTE.LEDGER_ID

and   XAH.APPLICATION_ID            = XAL.APPLICATION_ID

and   XE.EVENT_ID                   = XAH.EVENT_ID

and   XE.ENTITY_ID                  = XTE.ENTITY_ID

and   GIR.GL_SL_LINK_ID             = XAL.GL_SL_LINK_ID

and   GIR.GL_SL_LINK_TABLE          = XAL.GL_SL_LINK_TABLE

and   GJH.JE_SOURCE                 = 'Payables'
```

```
and     GIR.JE_BATCH_ID                     = GJB.JE_BATCH_ID

and     GIR.JE_HEADER_ID                    = GJH.JE_HEADER_ID

and     GJH.LEDGER_ID                       = XAH.LEDGER_ID

and     GJH.JE_HEADER_ID                    = GJL.JE_HEADER_ID

and     XAL.CODE_COMBINATION_ID             = GJL.CODE_COMBINATION_ID

and     XE.APPLICATION_ID                   = XTE.APPLICATION_ID(+)

and     XDL.AE_HEADER_ID                    = XAL.AE_HEADER_ID

and     XDL.AE_LINE_NUM                     = XAL.AE_LINE_NUM

and     XDL.APPLIED_TO_SOURCE_ID_NUM_1      = AIA.INVOICE_ID

and     XDL.SOURCE_DISTRIBUTION_ID_NUM_1 = AID.INVOICE_DISTRIBUTION_ID

and     AID.INVOICE_ID                      = AIA.INVOICE_ID

and     AIA.VENDOR_ID                       = APS.VENDOR_ID

and     xep.legal_entity_id                 = aia.legal_entity_id

and     AIA.INVOICE_NUM                     ='DS007'

--and    APS.VENDOR_NAME                     ='FRANCHISE TAX BOARD'

--and    AID.INVOICE_DISTRIBUTION_ID         ='24037'

and     AID.LINE_TYPE_LOOKUP_CODE           = 'ITEM'

and     AIA.PAYMENT_STATUS_FLAG             ='Y';
```

STANDARD DATA FIX

Just like we saw the importance of having a program developed to scan data corruptions and fix in Receivables, Payables can also be implemented with the same. A program to scan and fix standard Oracle data corruption would definitely save a lot of time for the organization.

Use Cases

Below are some the standard GDF's that can be added to the Master GDF Fix program

Invoice Validation is not picking invoices

In this issue, the invoice validation initially did not process the invoice but somehow ended up with updating the request id. If the invoices to be picking up for next validation, the request id needs to be removed. More details of the data fix is provided in the Oracle document id 1072774.1.

Query used to identify the issue as mentioned below

```
SELECT /*+ parallel(ai) */ ai.*,''N'' PROCESS_FLAG

                FROM ap_invoices_all ai

                    WHERE ai.validation_request_id IS NOT NULL

                    and ai.invoice_date between l_start_date and
l_end_Date

                    AND ai.validation_request_id > 0

                    AND ( EXISTS

                        ( SELECT 1  FROM fnd_concurrent_requests fcr

                          WHERE fcr.request_id =
ai.validation_request_id

                          AND fcr.phase_code = ''C'' )

                          OR NOT EXISTS

                        ( SELECT 1 FROM fnd_concurrent_requests fcr

                          WHERE fcr.request_id = ai.validation_request_id
)

                    )';
```

Invoices Stuck after PPR is terminated

This is a very useful GDF that is must for any organization that uses Oracle Payment. While working for one of the leading Global Retail company, we have utilized this fix a lot to release the stuck invoices for next batch. More details about this GDF is provided in the Document id 874862.1

```
    SELECT aisc.checkrun_id,

      aisc.check_date,

      aisc.checkrun_name,

      aisc.status ,

      aisc.request_id,

      COUNT(DISTINCT aps.invoice_id),

      COUNT(aps.invoice_id),

      ''y''

    FROM ap_inv_selection_criteria_all aisc,

        ap_payment_schedules_all aps

    WHERE aisc.checkrun_id = ' || l_checkrun_id || '

  AND   aps.checkrun_id = aisc.checkrun_id

  AND NOT EXISTS

    (SELECT ''Data in AP_SELECTED_INVOICES_ALL''

    FROM ap_selected_invoices_all asi

    WHERE asi.checkrun_id = aisc.checkrun_id

    )

  GROUP BY aisc.checkrun_id,

    aisc.check_date,

    aisc.checkrun_name,

    aisc.status,

    aisc.request_id
```

Duplicate AWT distribution

Sometime orphan AWT distributions are created during the payment process. Such duplicate AWT distributions should be deleted with a GDF. Oracle has provided a GDF to remove the orphan AWT distributions and more details are provided in the document 1188825.1

If the below query returns any data, then we have a possible orphan AWT distribution present in the system.

```
select aid.invoice_id,
        aid.invoice_distribution_id,
        aid.invoice_line_number,
        aid.distribution_line_number,
      aid.amount,
        aid.accounting_event_id,
        aid.posted_flag,
      aid.parent_reversal_id,
        aid.org_id,
      1 type,
      aid.awt_invoice_id  dup_awt_invoice_id
   from ap_invoice_distributions_all aid,
        ap_system_parameters_all asp,
        ap_invoice_lines_all ail,
        ap_invoices_all ai /* Bug 17311645 */
  where aid.line_type_lookup_code = ''AWT''
          and aid.awt_flag = ''A''
          and aid.historical_flag is null
          and aid.org_id = asp.org_id
      and aid.invoice_id = ail.invoice_id
          and aid.invoice_line_number = ail.line_number
          and asp.create_awt_dists_type = ''PAYMENT''
      and aid.awt_invoice_payment_id is null
          and ai.invoice_id = ail.invoice_id
          and not exists
        (
          select ''Invoice already withheld by AutoApproval''
          from ap_invoices_all ai
          where ai.invoice_id = aid.invoice_id
          and nvl(ai.awt_flag, ''N'') = ''Y''
        )  )';
```

CONCLUSION

Accounts Payable Automations:

The main intention of the RPA to Reduce or eliminate manual data entry, validation, and processing for invoices in your Accounts Payable department to get vendors paid faster and with fewer errors.

Payables Automation refers to the use of software and technology tools to replace everyday manual tasks, activities, and decisions related to invoice processing. This includes everything from extracting and validating header and line item data from invoice images, pairing PO items with your ERP, and assigning and routing invoices for approval.

Capture physical and digital invoices into ERP, ECM, or Intelligent Data Capture solution. Extract invoice header and detail data from invoice images using Intelligent Data Capture. Validate invoice data against vendor and PO tables, ERP data, or other accounting system. Export invoice image with validated invoice data to ECM or ERP for approvals. Assign and Route invoices to approvers with automatic notifications

Benefits with AP Automation

By using effective AP Automation process, organizations will be able to avoid costly delays and errors that are in repetitive in nature, while invoice processing. Substituting manual tasks, activities, and decisions, invoices are handled with accuracy and your AP Processors are free to focus on exceptions.

a. Get vendors paid faster with fewer errors and Create transparency and visibility into your invoice processing workflows
b. Measure solution and team efficiency, and identify bottlenecks. Qualify for early payment discounts and avoid late payment penalties. Simultaneously reduce costs and improve service levels

RPA IN CASH MANAGEMENT

OBJECTIVE

Objective of this chapter is to explain the importance of Oracle Cash Management, Why CM module is important in oracle to maintain the Reconciliation, cash positioning and cash forecasting. we can plan our cash positioning based on this cash management process

INTRODUCTION – CASH MANAGEMENT

Oracle Cash Management is an enterprise cash management solution that helps you effectively manage and control your cash cycle. It provides comprehensive bank reconciliation and flexible cash forecasting. In this module we define and tracks all bank account information in a central place. Grants explicitly account access to multiple operating units/functions and users. Uses Multi-Org Access and UMX-based security. Provides ownership of bank accounts by legal entities with the option to grant account use to Operating Unit (Payables, Receivables), Legal Entity (Treasury), and Business Group (Payroll).

The main important activity is to have enough cash on hand at the right time in order to fund core business operations, if we don't have operating cash is on hand and it will be impacting our business a lot. Oracle Cash Management gives you direct visibility into expected cash needs and forecasted cash receipts (by running cash required report). You can quickly analyze enterprise-wide cash requirements and currency exposures, ensuring liquidity and optimal use of cash resources for running the business without any last-minute challenges

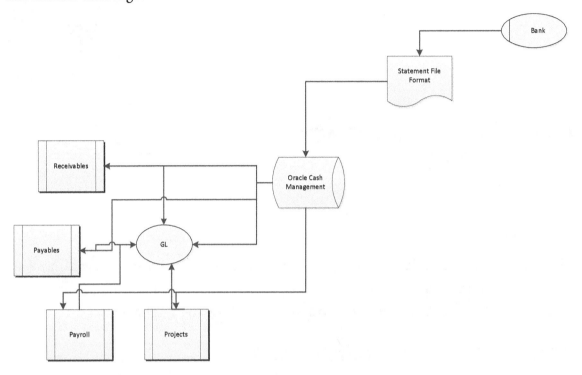

Oracle cash management Process.

We do have a Oracle Cash forecasting functionality, which can estimate the cash movement for multiple periods and for multiple currencies, by looking at the cash inflows and cash outflows. We can have multiple cash forecasting templates to meet multiple requirements.

With the Cash Management module you can

> We can centralize our cash management
> Bank Account Transfers can be easily maintained. Cash pooling activity in between the internal bank accounts
> It will help the cash positioning accuracy
> Automatically do the reconciliation for the statement line with its sub-ledger transaction (Receipt or Payment)
> Cash pooling can be done.

- o Notional cash pooling
- o Physical cash pooling

Bank Account Balances and Interest Calculation

Centralizes balances and interest. Tracks balances of all internal bank accounts in a single location. Reports on the accumulated bank account interest. Single place to maintain balances for all internal bank accounts. Flexible tool to calculate interest due.

Bank Account Transfers

Allows creating, approving, settling and accounting for cash transfers between internal bank accounts. Uses with Cash Pools, Zero Balance Accounts (ZBA) and Cash Leveling activities

Cash pooling

Is a cash management technique aimed at optimizing the balances of the internal bank accounts held at one or several banks is usually performed on a daily basis? Can be done by transaction or by total net end-of-day balances?

- Notional Cash Pools: Consist of one concentration account and multiple sub-accounts. Are used for cash leveling similar to zero balancing without the actual funds movement.
- Physical Cash Pools: Consist of one or two concentration accounts and multiple subaccounts with funds transfer rules specified. Are used for cash leveling wherein you can initiate fund transfers or mirror outsourced cash pools.

Bank Statements

Cash Management maintains information for each bank statement you want to reconcile. You can use the Cash Management Bank Statement Open Interface to load bank statement information supplied by your bank, or you can enter and update bank statements manually. The system retains all bank statement information for audit and reference purposes, until you purge it.

Bank Statement Transaction Codes

Bank statement lines are coded to identify the type of transaction the line represents. Since each bank might use a different set of transaction codes, you need to map each code your bank uses.

How is the data from Cash Management important?

Cash is the lifeblood of a business and a business needs to generate enough cash from its activities so that it can meet its expenses and have enough left over to repay investors and grow the business. While a company can fudge its earnings, its cash flow provides an idea about its real health.

Even if a company is making a profit, by making more revenue than it incurs in expenses, it will have to manage its cash flow correctly to be successful. The cash that a company generates from its operations is tied to its core business activities and provides the best opportunities for cash flow management.

Cash management and cash flow are two of the scariest things for any business to control. Improper cash management can lead to excessive debt or even bankruptcy. Lack of cash management can potentially put small businesses out of business because they do not have good cash management.

Businesses that have poor cash management can fall behind in debt and monthly operational expenses, making it extremely hard to recoup stability. Sometimes when things are very rough   lack of cash flow can prevent the processing of payroll. Employees will not work if they do not get paid. If your cash flow issues get to that point the business has little chance to recover.

ROBOTIC PROCESS AUTOMATION IN CASH MANAGEMENT

In the earlier session we have discussed about importance of cash management and what are the significance of various activities within cash management that contribute to an efficient cash flow to the company. One of the Boston Consulting Group Publication[1] states that by systematic incorporating the RPA into the cash management process can increase the production of the company and also boost the ability to generate insights.

Bill Gates once said that automation applied to an efficient operation will magnify the efficiency. It is certainly true for automated cash management. It's fast,

Now let us see how RPA can contribute an efficient cash management.

INTERNAL BANK API

Internal bank accounts are the bank accounts, which are owned by the company/legal entity, for the bank accounts for which you are the account holder. Oracle Receivables uses internal bank accounts to receive payments from customers. Oracle Payables uses internal bank accounts to disburse funds to the suppliers.

We do have an oracle standard API (CE_BANK_PUB.CREATE_BANK_ACCT) to create a internal bank accounts for the branch party id passed as an input parameter in oracle applications. API uses the BANKACCT_REC_TYPE record to pass the input values. On successful creation of bank account, the API returns the bank account id along with the information /error messages. The API returns a null bank account id if the bank branch is not created. In oracle release 12, all the internal bank accounts will be stored in CE_BANK_ACCOUNTS table.

```
SET SERVEROUTPUT ON;

DECLARE

    p_init_msg_list    VARCHAR2 (200);

    p_acct_rec         apps.ce_bank_pub.bankacct_rec_type;

    x_acct_id          NUMBER;

    x_return_status    VARCHAR2 (200);

    x_msg_count        NUMBER;

    x_msg_data         VARCHAR2 (200);

    p_count            NUMBER;
```

```
BEGIN

    p_init_msg_list := NULL;

    -- HZ_PARTIES.PARTY_ID BANK BRANCH

    p_acct_rec.branch_id := 8056;

    -- HZ_PARTIES.PARTY_ID BANK

    p_acct_rec.bank_id := 8042;

    -- HZ_PARTIES.PARTY_ID ORGANIZATION

    p_acct_rec.account_owner_org_id := 23273;

    -- HZ_PARTIES.PARTY_ID Person related to ABOVE ORGANIZATION

    p_acct_rec.account_owner_party_id := 2041;


    p_acct_rec.account_classification := 'INTERNAL';

    p_acct_rec.bank_account_name := 'Test Bank Acount';

    p_acct_rec.bank_account_num := 14256789;

    p_acct_rec.currency := 'USD';

    p_acct_rec.start_date := SYSDATE;

    p_acct_rec.end_date := NULL;


    CE_BANK_PUB.CREATE_BANK_ACCT

                    (p_init_msg_list      => p_init_msg_list,

                     p_acct_rec           => p_acct_rec,

                     x_acct_id            => x_acct_id,

                     x_return_status      => x_return_status,

                     x_msg_count          => x_msg_count,
```

```
                  x_msg_data              => x_msg_data

              );

  DBMS_OUTPUT.put_line ('X_ACCT_ID = ' || x_acct_id);

   DBMS_OUTPUT.put_line ('X_RETURN_STATUS = ' || x_return_status);

   DBMS_OUTPUT.put_line ('X_MSG_COUNT = ' || x_msg_count);

   DBMS_OUTPUT.put_line ('X_MSG_DATA = ' || x_msg_data);


   IF x_msg_count = 1

   THEN

       DBMS_OUTPUT.put_line ('x_msg_data ' || x_msg_data);

   ELSIF x_msg_count > 1

   THEN

       LOOP

          p_count := p_count + 1;

          x_msg_data      :=      fnd_msg_pub.get      (fnd_msg_pub.g_next,
fnd_api.g_false);


          IF x_msg_data IS NULL

          THEN

              EXIT;

          END IF;

          DBMS_OUTPUT.put_line ('Message' || p_count || ' ---' ||
x_msg_data);

       END LOOP;

    END IF;
```

```
END;
```

We do have a standard API (CE_BANK_PUB.UPDATE_BANK_ACCT) for bank Account update:

If we want to do any updates to the internal bank accounts by using this update script to update the details in the Bank Account.

```
SET SERVEROUTPUT ON;

DECLARE

    p_init_msg_list             VARCHAR2 (200);

    p_acct_rec                  apps.ce_bank_pub.bankacct_rec_type;

    p_object_version_number     NUMBER;

    x_return_status             VARCHAR2 (200);

    x_msg_count                 NUMBER;

    x_msg_data                  VARCHAR2 (200);

    p_count                     NUMBER;

BEGIN

    p_init_msg_list := NULL;

    p_acct_rec.bank_account_id := 92001;

    -- HZ_PARTIES.PARTY_ID BANK BRANCH

    p_acct_rec.branch_id := 9016;

    -- HZ_PARTIES.PARTY_ID BANK

    p_acct_rec.bank_id := 8042;

    -- HZ_PARTIES.PARTY_ID ORGANIZATION

    p_acct_rec.account_owner_org_id := 23273;

    -- HZ_PARTIES.PARTY_ID Person related to ABOVE ORGANIZATION

    p_acct_rec.account_owner_party_id := 2041;
```

```
p_acct_rec.account_classification := 'INTERNAL';

p_acct_rec.bank_account_name := 'internal Acount';

p_acct_rec.bank_account_num := 9908901;

p_acct_rec.currency := 'INR';

p_acct_rec.start_date := SYSDATE;

p_acct_rec.end_date := NULL;

p_object_version_number := 1;

ce_bank_pub.update_bank_acct
                        (p_init_msg_list                          =>
p_init_msg_list,

                    p_acct_rec                    => p_acct_rec,

                    p_object_version_number                       =>
p_object_version_number,

                    x_return_status                               =>
x_return_status,

                    x_msg_count               => x_msg_count,

                    x_msg_data               => x_msg_data
                    );
DBMS_OUTPUT.put_line (    'P_OBJECT_VERSION_NUMBER = '

                    || p_object_version_number
                    );
DBMS_OUTPUT.put_line ('X_RETURN_STATUS = ' || x_return_status);

DBMS_OUTPUT.put_line ('X_MSG_COUNT = ' || x_msg_count);

DBMS_OUTPUT.put_line ('X_MSG_DATA = ' || x_msg_data);


IF x_msg_count = 1
```

```
    THEN

        DBMS_OUTPUT.put_line ('x_msg_data ' || x_msg_data);

    ELSIF x_msg_count > 1

    THEN

        LOOP

            p_count := p_count + 1;

            x_msg_data     :=     fnd_msg_pub.get     (fnd_msg_pub.g_next,
fnd_api.g_false);


            IF x_msg_data IS NULL

            THEN

                EXIT;

            END IF;


            DBMS_OUTPUT.put_line   ('Message' ||  p_count  || '  ---'  ||
x_msg_data);

        END LOOP;

    END IF;

END;

/
```

BANK STATEMENT LOADER

In oracle cash management, we have a standard open interface for loading electronic bank statement files into the bank statement tables. Normally Bank Statement Open Interface contains two interface tables process and one import program. In generally bank statement tables contains information about the bank statement header and bank statement lines and the Bank Statement Import program transfers information from the open interface tables to the bank statement tables.

In Oracle Release 12 to simplify the implementation of Oracle Cash Management, the Bank Statement Open Interface is improved to offer a complete solution for loading bank statement information from an external file (we used to receive this stamen file from the bank). Using the new Bank Statement Loader feature in release 12, Statements can be quickly, easily and accurately loaded from BAI2 and SWIFT940 bank statement files into the Bank Statement Open Interface tables without any programming. The Bank Statement Loader also supports user-defined formats like French EDIFACT. Once data is populated into the open interface tables, the Bank Statement Import program is used to transfer the data to the base bank statement tables.

Bank Statement interface process

To accomplish this bank statement integration we need the below configuration in application. Major and very most important setup is,

a. We should have the bank account configured in the oracle apps.

b. **Bank Transaction Codes:** If we have decided to use electronic bank statements or use Cash Management's Auto Reconciliation functionality, Transaction codes setup has to define for each bank account. Transaction codes will be provided by the bank account and the transaction codes are used to identify different types of transactions on the bank statements. Define the bank transaction code for each code that you expect to receive from your bank with effective date range fields, Start Date and End Date, so that you can make a bank transaction code inactive. We will be having Payment, Receipts, NSF..etc all types of transaction codes which will be provided by bank.

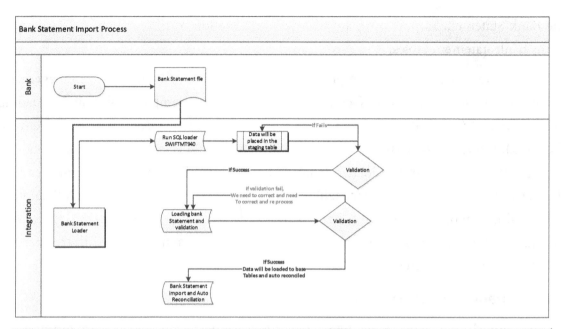

Type		Code	Description	Domain	Family	Sub Family	Effective Dates Start	End	
Receipt	▼	100C	Customer Payme						
Payment	▼	100D	Customer Payme						
Receipt	▼	101C	Request for Trans						
Payment	▼	101D	Request for Trans						
Receipt	▼	103C	Single Customer						
Receipt	▼	190C	Advice of Charges						
Payment	▼	190D	Advice of Charges						
Receipt	▼	191C	Request for Paym						
Payment	▼	191D	Request for Paym						

c. **Define Mapping Rule.**

Bank Statement Mapping in Cash Management module is also a major setups as it is the one, which identify the statement positioning. Always, it is a good idea to copy the seeded mappings to your own so that we can modify it easily. When you navigate to the statements form, it will prompt you to find a mapping. Cancel that dialog. When the find window disappears, give your new format a name and description. Use the existing control file and supply the desired date format. Define the precision and choose the appropriate format type. Then click on Populate and save. This will copy the default mapping to your new name. Then we need to amend the values which we want to modify or amend.

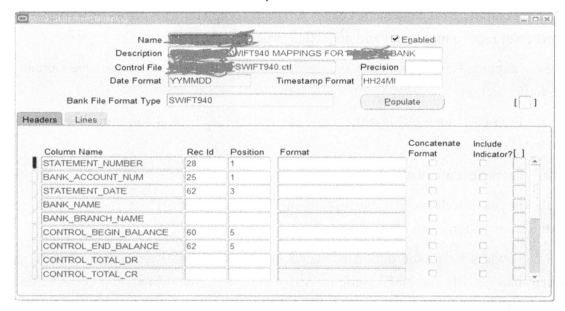

We need to place the statement file in the specified path, for example – XX/UK/CE/inbound/stamen.txt

d. We need to submit the Bank Statement Import program

While submitting the bank statement import program, we will be having multiple parameters as below

Process Option - "Load". Or "Load and Import" or "Load, Import, and AutoReconciliation"

The Bank Statement Loader program can be executed in one of these three modes:

1. Load
2. Load and Import
3. Load, Import and Auto Reconciliation

In Option 1 is only to run the loader program.

In option 2, the Bank Statement Import program starts after the Bank Statement Loader completes successfully.

In option 3, both the Bank Statement Import program and the Auto Reconciliation programs launched after successful completion of the Bank Statement Loader program. In either case, if the Bank Statement Loader program completes with errors or warnings, the concurrent request terminates and no further process is started.

Mapping Name – we need to select the bank statement which we have defined in the earlier section.

Data File Name - This is the name of the data file. Typical convention is to use the .dat extension.

Example: statement.dat

If you selected either the option of "Load and Import" or "Load,Import, and AutoReconciliation", enter the GL Date.

If you selected the option of "Load, Import and AutoReconciliation", enter the Receivables Activity and NSF Handling. Also enter the Payment Method if you specified a bank account number.

If multiple files have been loaded, but only one is to be imported, use Statement Date or Statement Number range parameters to limit the import job.

We will also see the concurrent jobs which has been kicked off by using this process

a. When you run SQL loader program It will place the data into the CE_STMT_INT_TMP table.

b. Load bank Statement Data – this program will take care of loading the statement data from the temp to the interface tables (CE_STATEMENT_ HEADERS_INTERFACE and CE_STATEMENT_LINES_INTERFACE tables)

c. Bank Statement Loader Execution Report – this is a just a report output of the previous job

d. Bank Statement Import – this program will import the data into the base tables (CE_STATEMENT_HEADERS_INTERFACE and CE_STATEMENT_LINES_ INTERFACE tables into the CE_STATEMENT_HEADERS and CE_STATEMENT _LINES tables)

e. Auto Reconciliation- Auto Reconciliation program is used to reconcile the imported the bank statement lines with the outstanding AP and AR transactions

f. Auto Reconciliation execution report - Now the same report shows exceptions in matching up the imported bank statement transactions with the existing AP, AR, GL, Payroll and Miscellaneous transactions in the system. It gives descriptive reasons why the line was not able to be reconciled automatically.

7

RPA IN FIXED ASSETS

OBJECTIVE

Objective of this chapter is to explain the importance of Oracle Fixed Asset Module, Why this module is important for the Client's Management/Leadership team and what is the impact of delayed data input/Process delay/Manual work/any bottlenecks. How a company can increase the efficiency of processes by incorporating the Robotic Automation in their company?. Share the experience from actual Doyensys clients.

INTRODUCTION - FIXED ASSETS

A fixed asset is a long-term tangible piece of property or equipment that a firm owns and uses in its operations to generate income. Fixed assets are not expected to be consumed or converted into cash within a year. Fixed assets most commonly appear on the balance sheet as property, plant, and equipment (PP&E). They are also referred to as capital assets.

How a Fixed Asset Works

A company's balance sheet statement consists of its assets, liabilities, and shareholders' equity. Assets are divided into current assets and noncurrent assets, the difference for which lies in their useful lives. Current assets are typically liquid assets which will be converted into cash in less than a year. Noncurrent assets refer to assets and property owned by a business which are not easily converted to cash. The different categories of noncurrent assets include fixed assets, intangible assets, long-term investments, and deferred charges.

A fixed asset is bought for production or supply of goods or services, for rental to third parties, or for use in the organization. The term "fixed" translates to the fact that these assets will not be used up or sold within the accounting year. A fixed asset typically has a physical form and is reported on the balance sheet as property, plant, and equipment (PP&E).

When a company acquires or disposes of a fixed asset, this is recorded on the cash flow statement under the cash flow from investing activities. The purchase of fixed assets represents a cash outflow to the company, while a sale is a cash inflow. If the value of the asset falls below its net book value, the asset is subject to an impairment write-down. This means that its recorded value on the balance sheet is adjusted downward to reflect that its overvalued compared to the market value.

When a fixed asset has reached the end of its useful life, it is usually disposed of by selling it for a salvage value, which is the estimated value of the asset if it was broken down and sold in parts. In some cases, the asset may become obsolete and may no longer have a market for it, and will, therefore, be disposed of without receiving any payment in return. Either way, the fixed asset is written off the balance sheet as it is no longer in use by the company.

Special Considerations

Fixed assets lose value as they age. Because they provide long-term income, these assets are expensed differently than other items. Tangible assets are subject to periodic depreciation, as intangible assets are subject to amortization. A certain amount of an asset's costs is expensed annually. The asset's value decreases along with its depreciation amount on the company's balance sheet. The corporation can then match the asset's cost with its long-term value.

How a business depreciates an asset can cause its book value—the asset value that appears on the balance sheet—to differ from the current market value at which the asset could sell. Land cannot be depreciated unless it contains natural resources, in which case depletion would be recorded.

Fixed Assets vs. Current Assets

Both current assets and fixed assets appear on the balance sheet, with current assets meant to be used or converted to cash in the short-term (less than one year) and fixed assets meant to be utilized for the longer-term (greater than one year). Current assets include cash and cash equivalents, accounts receivable, inventory, and prepaid expenses. Fixed assets are depreciated, while current assets are not.

Fixed Assets vs. Noncurrent Assets

Fixed assets are a noncurrent asset. Other noncurrent assets include long-term investments and intangibles. Intangible assets are fixed assets, meant to be used over the long-term, but they lack physical existence. Examples of intangible assets include goodwill, copyrights, trademarks, and intellectual property. Meanwhile, long-term investments can include bond investments that will not be sold or mature within a year.

Benefits of Fixed Assets

Information about a corporation's assets helps create accurate financial reporting, business valuations, and thorough financial analysis. Investors and creditors use these reports to determine a company's financial health and to decide whether to buy shares in or lend money to the business. Because a company may use a range of accepted methods for recording, depreciating, and disposing of its assets, analysts need to study the notes on the corporation's financial statements to find out how the numbers were determined.

Fixed assets are particularly important to capital-intensive industries, such as manufacturing, that require large investments in PP&E. When a business is reporting persistently negative net cash flows for the purchase of fixed assets, this could be a strong indicator that the firm is in growth or investment mode.

Below are examples of fixed assets:

o   Vehicles such as company trucks
o   Office furniture
o   Machinery
o   Buildings
o   Land

Fixed assets are not readily liquid and cannot be easily converted into cash. They are not sold or consumed by a company. Instead, the asset is used to produce goods and services.

Fixed tangible assets can be depreciated over time to reduce the recorded cost of the asset. Most tangible assets, such as buildings, machinery, and equipment, can be depreciated. However, land cannot be depreciated because it cannot be depleted over time unless it is land containing natural resources.

Examples: An example of a company's fixed asset would be a company that produces and sells toys. The company purchases a new office building for $5 million along with machinery and equipment that costs a total of $500,000. The company projects using the building, machinery, and equipment for the next five years. These assets are considered fixed tangible assets because they have physical form, will have a useful life of more than one year, and will be used to generate revenue for the company.

RPA IN FIXED ASSETS

There are areas within Fixed assets or processes in Fixed Asset module can be made more efficient and error-free with the usage of RPA. Doyensys has worked on Automating FA module for many clients. Some of our use cases and solutions are provided below

DATA MIGRATION

There was a requirement from one of the leading FMCG and Health care company subdivision was migrating from Legacy to ORACLE. While moving assets from one location to another Location, Asset cost also transfer from one location to another and in same way they need to have the requirement fit in oracle also.

Analysis

After receiving the requirement we have started working on the standard and custom options to achieve the requirement from business and found one of the easy option is SLA customization by customizing the ADR for assets because Location is the one of the segment for them.

Solution

We have reviewed the standard oracle account derivation rule. It was built as below

- Company Segment derives from Expense account(Depreciation)
- Natural Account derives from Asset Category
- All segments derives from Book Controls(all other accounts)

To achieve this we have to derive the Location segment also. We built the rules as below.

Fixed Assets SLA Customization:

Additions

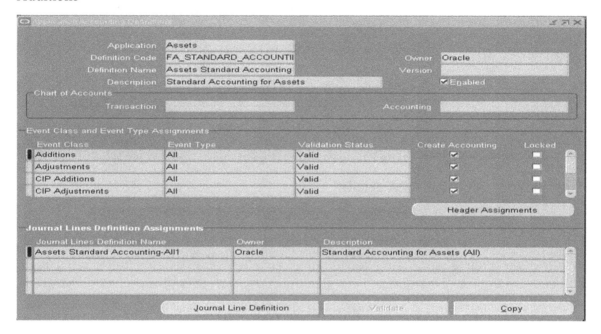

Click on Copy

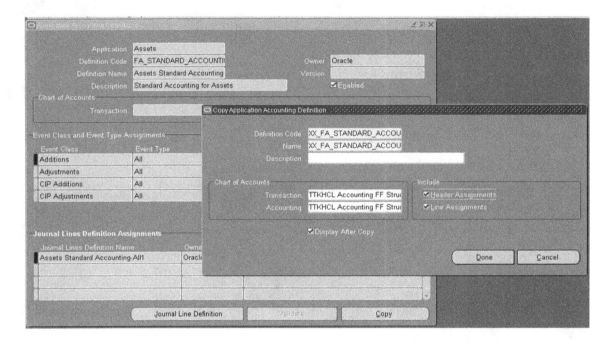

Enter the code, name and COA details

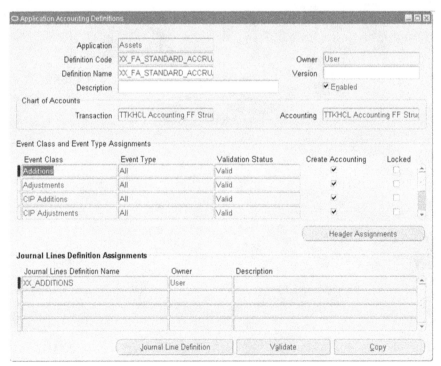

Click on Journal Line definitions.

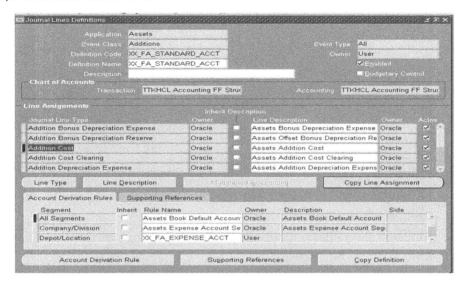

Click on Account Derivation Rule and then press down arrow

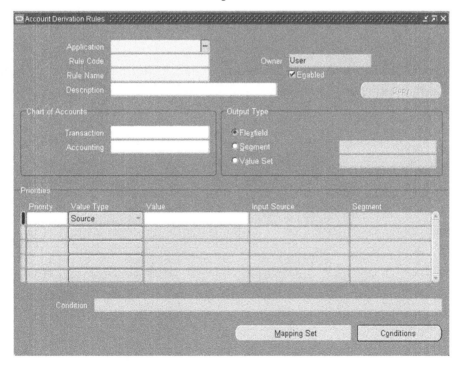

Enter the Application and Rule details

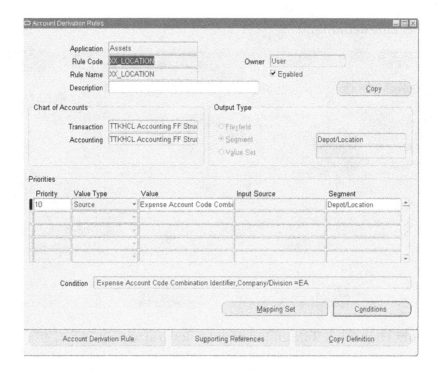

Click On Conditions

Note: we have restricted the data for Company Code EA. In future if the user need to have the same configuration for all entities, then remove this condition and Validate the AAD(Application Accounting Definition)

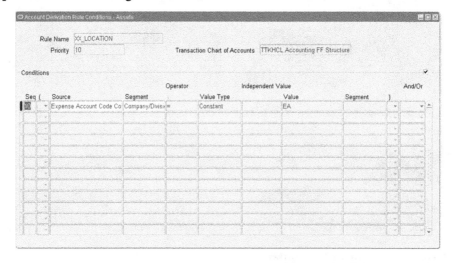

Add a new derivation rule and add the newly created ADR

Go back to AAD screen

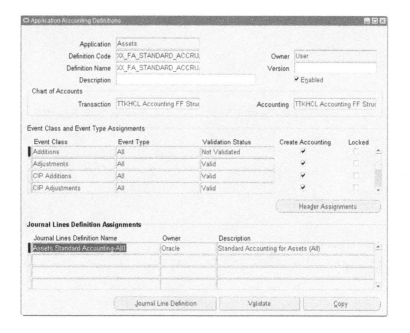

Add the newly created Journal line definition and Delete the seeded Journal line definition

by clicking into delete button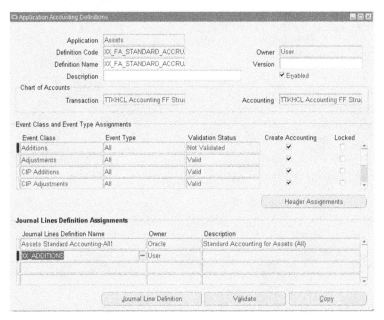

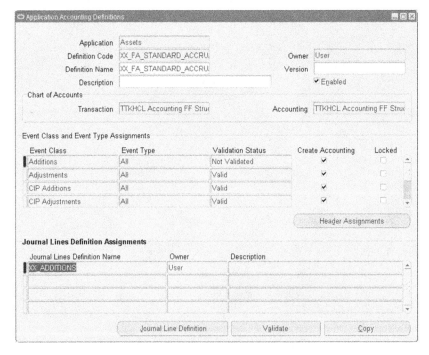

Perform the same setups for other event classes also.

ASSET TRANSFER IN EAM

This topic related to the companies using Oracle Fixed assets and Enterprise asset management. There is a common requirement for company's using Oracle FA and EAM together in their business areas is whenever any asset transferred in EAM from one location to another should also be reflected and vice versa.

Analysis

There are few workarounds and Solutions available to achieve this. Oracle also has provides solution to achieve this using Oracle asset tracking a separate module which incur licensing cost to company. Below are the brief about solution available as per oracle note(1235824.1)

Why Location changes in FA (Fixed Assets) is not reflected in EAM (Enterprise Asset Management) and vice-versa?

Solution as per oracle.

The synchronized check-box is applicable only if our customers are using Asset Tracking (OAT) product along with EAM.

Asset Tracking is mandatory for FA synchronization. eAM Asset (and also OAT instances) represent the physical face of the Asset, whereas FA represents the financial face of the asset. You could move the eAM/OAT Asset from one location to another through deployment transactions, or any of the standard inventory transactions or even a UI location update. All these should get picked by the OAT move concurrent program and interfaced to FA.

This flag (synchronized checkbox) -through OAT- helps in keeping the operational attributes of the Asset in sync with the financial attributes of FA Number, when Assets move between locations.

You need to run OAT 's Interface Move Transaction concurrent program, to reflect these updates.

Synchronization Of Locations Between FA And EAM modules (Doc ID 1235824.1)

Usage Of Synchronized CheckBox In Define Asset Number Form? (Doc ID 786272.1)

Solution

We have applied this solution in one of the leading EPC Company, we built a custom Program to get the asset movement data from EAM and interface to FA as a Location change. Point of source is EAM for this company, so the asset movement will only flow from EAM to FA.

Prerequisites

- o FA installed
- o EAM Installed
- o FA Asset created
- o EAM asset created
- o FA asset tagged in EAM

  EAM asset tagging shown below.

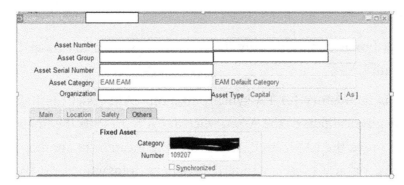

Logic Follows

Location flexfield of the assets (if Asset is moved to a location in India) to be updated as below:

- Country Segment – to be picked up from Country field from address of EAM Organization
- State Segment – to be picked up from Segment A of Material Account defined at EAM Organization

Depreciation Charge Account (if asset is moved to a location in India) to be updated as below:

- Country – to be picked up from SegmentA of Material Account defined at EAM Organization
- Cost Centre – to be picked up from SegmentC of Material Account defined at EAM Organization
- Location - to be picked up from SegmentB of Material Account defined at EAM Organization

Location flexfield of the assets (if Asset is moved to a location outside India) to be updated as below:

- Country Segment – to be picked up from Country field from address of EAM Organization
- State Segment – to be picked up from Segment A of Material Account defined at EAM Organization

  a. Depreciation Charge Account (if asset is moved to a location outside India) to be updated as below:

    - Entity – to be picked up from a lookup defined for the purpose
    - Cost Centre – to be picked up from a lookup defined for the purpose
    - Location - to be picked up from a lookup defined for the purpose

1. An alert will be generated to notify users for the FA assets transferred basis location information at EAM Asset.
2. An alert will be generated to notify users upon movement of EAM assets which are not linked to FA Assets.

Code follows

```
CREATE OR REPLACE PACKAGE apps.xxfa_asset_tran_eam_pkg
AS
    PROCEDURE xx_eam_fa_asset (
        errbuf          OUT     VARCHAR2,
        retcode         OUT     VARCHAR2,
        p_ledger_id     IN      NUMBER,
        p_eam_org       IN      VARCHAR2,
```

```
    p_book_name    IN        VARCHAR2
);
FUNCTION xx_create_ccid (
    p_segment1    IN    VARCHAR2,
    p_segment2    IN    VARCHAR2,
    p_segment3    IN    VARCHAR2,
    p_segment4    IN    VARCHAR2,
    p_segment5    IN    VARCHAR2,
    p_segment6    IN    VARCHAR2,
    p_segment7    IN    VARCHAR2,
    p_ou_name     IN    NUMBER
)
    RETURN NUMBER;


FUNCTION xx_create_faloc_fun (
    p_loc_seg1    VARCHAR2,
    p_loc_seg2    VARCHAR2,
    p_loc_seg3    VARCHAR2
)
    RETURN NUMBER;
END xxfa_asset_tran_eam_pkg;
/


CREATE OR REPLACE PACKAGE BODY apps.xxfa_asset_tran_eam_pkg
IS
    PROCEDURE xx_eam_fa_asset (
        errbuf          OUT       VARCHAR2,
        retcode         OUT       VARCHAR2,
        p_ledger_id     IN        NUMBER,
        p_eam_org       IN        VARCHAR2,
        p_book_name     IN        VARCHAR2
    )
```

```
AS

    lc_flag                VARCHAR2 (1);
    lc_error_msg           VARCHAR2 (200);
    lc_org_code            VARCHAR2 (3);
    lc_ou_id               NUMBER;
    lc_locinfo             VARCHAR2 (100);
    lc_p_number            VARCHAR2 (240);
    lc_locid               NUMBER;
    lc_assginid            NUMBER;
    lc_ccid                NUMBER;
    lc_did                 NUMBER;
    lc_trans_units         NUMBER;
    lc_seg1                VARCHAR2 (25);
    lc_seg2                VARCHAR2 (25);
    lc_seg3                VARCHAR2 (25);
    lc_seg4                VARCHAR2 (25);
    lc_seg5                VARCHAR2 (25);
    lc_seg6                VARCHAR2 (25);
    lc_seg7                VARCHAR2 (25);
    lc_loc_seg1            VARCHAR2 (100);
    lc_loc_seg2            VARCHAR2 (100);
    lc_loc_seg3            VARCHAR2 (100);
    lc_new_ccid            NUMBER;
    lc_new_loc_id          NUMBER;
    lc_user_id             NUMBER                    :=
fnd_global.user_id;
    lc_resp_id             NUMBER                    :=
fnd_global.resp_id;
    lc_resp_appl_id        NUMBER                :=
fnd_global.resp_appl_id;
    l_stat                 VARCHAR2 (100);
    lc_return_status       VARCHAR2 (1);
    lc_mesg_count          NUMBER;
```

171

```
        lc_msg_count          NUMBER                              := 0;
        lc_mesg               VARCHAR2 (512);
        lc_msg_data           VARCHAR2 (4000);
        v_error_msg           VARCHAR2 (1000);
        lcfrom_exp_acct       VARCHAR2 (240);
        lcto_exp_acct         VARCHAR2 (240);
        lcfrm_loc             VARCHAR2 (240);
        lcto_loc              VARCHAR2 (240);
        asset_dist_tbl_type   fa_api_types.asset_dist_tbl_type;
        trans_rec_type        fa_api_types.trans_rec_type;
        asset_hdr_rec_type    fa_api_types.asset_hdr_rec_type;


--Cursor Declaration
        CURSOR lcu_eam_cur
        IS
            SELECT   cii.instance_id, cii.instance_number,
cii.serial_number,
                    cii.location_id, rsl.from_organization_id,
                    rsl.to_organization_id,
                    ood.organization_name from_org_name,
                    ood1.organization_name to_org_name,
                    ood1.organization_code to_org_code, rsl.item_id,
                    rsl.quantity_shipped, fa.asset_id,
fa.asset_number,
                    ood1.set_of_books_id
              FROM csi_item_instances cii,
                    csi_i_assets cia,
                    fa_additions fa,
                    fa_books fb,
                    rcv_shipment_headers rsh,
                    rcv_shipment_lines rsl,
                    mtl_supply ms,
```

```
            rcv_routing_headers rcvrh,
            hr_locations_all_tl hl,
            mtl_system_items msi,
            mtl_system_items msi1,
            mtl_units_of_measure mum,
            org_organization_definitions ood,
            org_organization_definitions ood1
        WHERE 1 = 1
--              AND rsh.receipt_source_code = 'INVENTORY'
--              AND ms.supply_type_code = 'SHIPMENT'
            AND ms.shipment_header_id(+) = rsh.shipment_header_id
            AND rsh.shipment_header_id = rsl.shipment_header_id
            AND rsh.ship_to_location_id = hl.location_id(+)
            AND hl.LANGUAGE(+) = USERENV ('LANG')
            AND rsl.routing_header_id =
rcvrh.routing_header_id(+)
            AND mum.unit_of_measure(+) = rsl.unit_of_measure
            AND msi.organization_id(+) = rsl.to_organization_id
            AND msi.inventory_item_id(+) = rsl.item_id
            AND msi1.organization_id(+) =
rsl.from_organization_id
            AND msi1.inventory_item_id(+) = rsl.item_id
            AND ood.organization_id = rsl.from_organization_id
            AND ms.shipment_line_id(+) = rsl.shipment_line_id
            AND cii.inventory_item_id = rsl.item_id
            AND ood1.organization_id = rsl.to_organization_id
            AND cii.instance_id = cia.instance_id(+)
            AND cia.fa_asset_id = fa.asset_id(+)
            AND fa.asset_id = fb.asset_id
            AND fb.date_ineffective IS NULL
            -- AND cii.instance_number = 'CC1263'
            AND ood1.set_of_books_id = p_ledger_id
```

```
                AND ood1.organization_code =

                                NVL (p_eam_org,
ood1.organization_code)

             AND fb.book_type_code = NVL (p_book_name,
fb.book_type_code)

                 -- AND TRUNC (rsh.last_update_date) = TRUNC
(SYSDATE)

             -- AND TRUNC (cii.last_update_date) = TRUNC (SYSDATE)

             AND cii.attribute30 IS NULL

        GROUP BY cii.instance_id,

                 cii.instance_number,

                 cii.serial_number,

                 cii.location_id,

                 rsl.from_organization_id,

                 rsl.to_organization_id,

                 ood.organization_name,

                 ood1.organization_name,

                 ood1.organization_code,

                 rsl.item_id,

                 rsl.quantity_shipped,

                 fa.asset_id,

                 fa.asset_number,

                 ood1.set_of_books_id,

                 cii.attribute30;

   BEGIN

     fnd_file.put_line (apps.fnd_file.output,

                   ('User ID ' || ' ' || lc_user_id
                   )
                   );

     fnd_file.put_line (apps.fnd_file.output,

                   ('Responsibility ID ' || ' ' || lc_resp_id
                   )
                   );
```

```
fnd_file.put_line (apps.fnd_file.output,
                    (   'Responsibility Application ID '
                     || ' '
                     || lc_resp_appl_id
                    )
                  );


--Initialize profile values
     BEGIN
        fnd_global.apps_initialize (user_id         =>
lc_user_id,
                                    resp_id         =>
lc_resp_id,
                                    resp_appl_id    =>
lc_resp_appl_id
                                  );

     END;


     FOR lcu_data IN lcu_eam_cur
     LOOP
--Variable Assign
        lc_flag := 'N';
        lc_error_msg := NULL;


/* Project number verification*/
        BEGIN
           SELECT proj.segment1
             INTO lc_p_number
             FROM hr_organization_units org,
                  pa_project_statuses ps,
                  pa_project_statuses ppsf,
                  pa_lookups lk1,
                  pa_distribution_rules rule,
```

```
                    pa_billing_cycles bill,

                    pa_project_types TYPE,

                    pa_projects_all proj,

                    pa_operating_units_v pou

             WHERE 'Y' IN (SELECT pa_security.allow_query
(proj.project_id)

                          FROM SYS.DUAL)

                 AND proj.carrying_out_organization_id =
org.organization_id

                 AND proj.project_status_code =
ps.project_status_code

                 AND proj.funding_approval_status_code =
ppsf.project_status_code(+)

                 AND proj.pm_product_code = lk1.lookup_code(+)

                 AND lk1.lookup_type(+) = 'PM_PRODUCT_CODE'

                 AND proj.distribution_rule =
rule.distribution_rule(+)

                 AND proj.billing_cycle_id = bill.billing_cycle_id(+)

                 AND proj.project_type = TYPE.project_type

                 AND ps.status_type = 'PROJECT'

                 AND TYPE.org_id = proj.org_id

                 AND pou.org_id = proj.org_id

                 AND org.NAME = lcu_data.to_org_name;
--'QIND01-CWS-Equipment Spares Store, BANMORE';
        EXCEPTION

          WHEN OTHERS

          THEN

            lc_flag := 'E';

            lc_error_msg :=

                 lc_error_msg

            || '-'

            || 'Project Number Not Avilable For Given
Organization : '

            || lcu_data.to_org_code;
```

```
        -- fnd_file.put_line (apps.fnd_file.output, lc_error_msg);
        END;


/* country and location checking verification*/
        BEGIN
            SELECT country || loc_information16,
ood.organization_code,
                ood.operating_unit
            INTO lc_locinfo, lc_org_code,
                lc_ou_id
            FROM hr_locations_all hl,
org_organization_definitions ood
            WHERE 1 = 1
                AND inventory_organization_id = ood.organization_id
                AND inventory_organization_id =
lcu_data.to_organization_id;
        EXCEPTION
            WHEN OTHERS
            THEN
                lc_flag := 'E';
                lc_error_msg :=
                            lc_error_msg || '-' || 'Invalid County
And State';
        --fnd_file.put_line (apps.fnd_file.output, lc_error_msg);
        END;


/*project and location ccid available or not checking */
        BEGIN
            SELECT dis.location_id, dis.assigned_to,
dis.distribution_id,
                dis.units_assigned, dis.code_combination_id,
                gcc.segment1, gcc.segment2, gcc.segment3,
gcc.segment4,
                gcc.segment5, gcc.segment6, gcc.segment7
```

```
            INTO lc_locid, lc_assginid, lc_did,
                 lc_trans_units, lc_ccid,
                 lc_seg1, lc_seg2, lc_seg3, lc_seg4,
                 lc_seg5, lc_seg6, lc_seg7
          FROM fa_additions_b ass,
               fa_distribution_history dis,
               gl_code_combinations gcc
         WHERE ass.asset_id = lcu_data.asset_id
           AND ass.asset_id = dis.asset_id
           AND dis.date_ineffective IS NULL
           AND gcc.code_combination_id =
dis.code_combination_id;
        EXCEPTION
           WHEN OTHERS
           THEN
             lc_flag := 'E';
             lc_error_msg :=
                   lc_error_msg
               || '-'
               || 'Given Asset ID Is Not Available : '
               || lcu_data.asset_id;
        --fnd_file.put_line (apps.fnd_file.output, lc_error_msg);
        END;


--Check new CCID is available or not
        BEGIN
           SELECT code_combination_id
             INTO lc_new_ccid
             FROM gl_code_combinations_kfv
            WHERE concatenated_segments =
                   lc_seg1
               || '.'
```

```
                || REPLACE (lc_seg2, lc_seg2, lc_p_number)
                || '.'
                || lc_seg3
                || '.'
                || lc_seg4
                || '.'
                || REPLACE (lc_seg5, lc_seg5, lc_locinfo)
                || '.'
                || lc_seg6
                || '.'
                || lc_seg7;
        EXCEPTION
            WHEN NO_DATA_FOUND
            THEN
--Call CCID Creation Function
            --fnd_file.put_line (apps.fnd_file.output,  ' ------
- Calling CCID Validation -------');
            lc_new_ccid :=
                xx_create_ccid (lc_seg1,
                                 lc_p_number,
                                 lc_org_code,
                                 lc_seg4,
                                 lc_locinfo,
                                 lc_seg6,
                                 lc_seg7,
                                 lc_ou_id
                                 );
        WHEN OTHERS
        THEN
            lc_error_msg := 'Error While Checking CCID ' ||
lc_ccid;
        END;
```

```
/* Validating for Asset Location */
        BEGIN
            SELECT fl.segment1, fl.segment2, fl.segment3
                INTO lc_loc_seg1, lc_loc_seg2, lc_loc_seg3
                FROM fa_locations fl              --,
fa_distribution_history fdh
                WHERE 1 = 1 AND fl.location_id = lc_locid;
        EXCEPTION
            WHEN OTHERS
            THEN
                lc_flag := 'E';
                lc_error_msg := lc_error_msg || '-' || 'Segments Not
Match';
        --fnd_file.put_line (apps.fnd_file.output, lc_error_msg);
        END;

/* Validating for New Asset Location */
        BEGIN
            SELECT location_id
                INTO lc_new_loc_id
                FROM fa_locations_kfv fl
            WHERE 1 = 1
                AND concatenated_segments =
                        lc_loc_seg1 || '.' || lc_locinfo || '.' ||
lc_p_number;
        -- fnd_file.put_line (apps.fnd_file.output,'The New
Location ID Details Is '|| lc_new_loc_id);
        EXCEPTION
            WHEN NO_DATA_FOUND
            THEN
                lc_new_loc_id :=
                    xx_create_faloc_fun (lc_loc_seg1,
```

```
                                        lc_locinfo,
                                        lc_p_number
                                   );

        WHEN OTHERS
        THEN
            lc_flag := 'E';
            lc_error_msg :=
                lc_error_msg
             || '-'
             || 'Error While Validating Asset Location : '
             || lc_loc_seg1
             || '.'
             || lc_locinfo
             || '.'
             || lc_p_number
             || ' - '
             || SQLERRM;
    -- fnd_file.put_line (apps.fnd_file.output, lc_error_msg);
    END;


    BEGIN
        SELECT concatenated_segments
          INTO lcfrom_exp_acct
          FROM gl_code_combinations_kfv
         WHERE code_combination_id = lc_ccid;              --Old
Expense CCID
    EXCEPTION
        WHEN OTHERS
        THEN
            lcfrom_exp_acct := NULL;
    END;
```

```
        BEGIN
            SELECT concatenated_segments
              INTO lcto_exp_acct
              FROM gl_code_combinations_kfv
             WHERE code_combination_id = lc_new_ccid;          --Old
Expense CCID
        EXCEPTION
            WHEN OTHERS
            THEN
                lcto_exp_acct := NULL;
        END;


        BEGIN
            SELECT concatenated_segments
              INTO lcfrm_loc
              FROM fa_locations_kfv
             WHERE location_id = lc_locid;                     --Old
Location ID
        EXCEPTION
            WHEN OTHERS
            THEN
                lcfrm_loc := NULL;
        END;


        BEGIN
            SELECT concatenated_segments
              INTO lcto_loc
              FROM fa_locations_kfv
             WHERE location_id = lc_new_loc_id;                --Old
Location ID
        EXCEPTION
            WHEN OTHERS
            THEN
```

```
        lcto_loc := NULL;

    END;


    IF lc_flag = 'N'
    THEN
        asset_hdr_rec_type.asset_id := lcu_data.asset_id;
        asset_dist_tbl_type (1).distribution_id := lc_did;
        asset_dist_tbl_type (1).transaction_units :=
lc_trans_units * -1;
        asset_dist_tbl_type (2).transaction_units :=
lc_trans_units;
--        asset_dist_tbl_type (2).assigned_to := lc_assginid;
        asset_dist_tbl_type (2).expense_ccid := lc_new_ccid;
        asset_dist_tbl_type (2).location_ccid := lc_new_loc_id;
--Calling API
        fa_transfer_pub.do_transfer
                    (p_api_version          => 1.0,
                    p_init_msg_list         =>
fnd_api.g_false,
                    p_commit                =>
fnd_api.g_false,
                    p_validation_level      =>
fnd_api.g_valid_level_full,
                    p_calling_fn            => NULL,
                    x_return_status         =>
lc_return_status,
                    x_msg_count             =>
lc_msg_count,
                    x_msg_data              => lc_msg_data,
                    px_trans_rec            =>
trans_rec_type,
                    px_asset_hdr_rec        =>
asset_hdr_rec_type,
                    px_asset_dist_tbl       =>
asset_dist_tbl_type
```

```
                            );
            lc_mesg_count := fnd_msg_pub.count_msg;


            IF lc_mesg_count > 0
            THEN
                lc_error_msg :=
                        CHR (10)
                    || SUBSTR (fnd_msg_pub.get (fnd_msg_pub.g_first,
                                                fnd_api.g_false
                                                ),
                                    1,
                                    250
                                    );
                fnd_file.put_line (apps.fnd_file.output,
lc_error_msg);


                FOR i IN 1 .. (lc_mesg_count - 1)
                LOOP
                    lc_error_msg :=
                        SUBSTR (fnd_msg_pub.get (fnd_msg_pub.g_next,
                                                fnd_api.g_false
                                                ),
                                    1,
                                    250
                                    );
                fnd_file.put_line (apps.fnd_file.output,
lc_error_msg);
                END LOOP;


                fnd_msg_pub.delete_msg ();
            END IF;
```

```
        IF (lc_return_status <> fnd_api.g_ret_sts_success)
THEN
    fnd_file.put_line (apps.fnd_file.output,
                        lcu_data.asset_id
                        || ' Asset Transfer Got Fail Due
To '
                        || lc_error_msg
                        );
        ELSE
    fnd_file.put_line (apps.fnd_file.output,
                        lcu_data.asset_id
                        || ' Asset Transfer Successfully
:'
                        || ' '
                        || 'From Exp Account :'
                        || ' '
                        || lcfrom_exp_acct
                        || ' , '
                        || 'To Exp Account :'
                        || ' '
                        || lcto_exp_acct
                        || ','
                        || 'AND'
                        || ' '
                        || 'From Location :'
                        || ' '
                        || lcfrm_loc
                        || ', '
                        || 'TO location:'
                        || ' '
                        || lcto_loc
                        );
```

185

```
            END IF;


        UPDATE csi_item_instances
           SET attribute30 = 'Asset Moved'
         WHERE serial_number = lcu_data.serial_number;


        COMMIT;
      END IF;
    END LOOP;
EXCEPTION
   WHEN OTHERS
   THEN
      fnd_file.put_line
           (apps.fnd_file.output,
              ' ------- Procedure XX_EAM_FA_ASSET Exception -
------'
              || SQLERRM
            );
   END xx_eam_fa_asset;


FUNCTION xx_create_ccid (
   p_segment1   IN   VARCHAR2,
   p_segment2   IN   VARCHAR2,
   p_segment3   IN   VARCHAR2,
   p_segment4   IN   VARCHAR2,
   p_segment5   IN   VARCHAR2,
   p_segment6   IN   VARCHAR2,
   p_segment7   IN   VARCHAR2,
   p_ou_name    IN   NUMBER
)
   RETURN NUMBER
IS
```

```
    lc_ccid              NUMBER;

    lc_coa_id            NUMBER;

    lc_coa_name          VARCHAR2 (100);

    lc_dynamic_insert    VARCHAR2 (1);

    lc_delimiter         VARCHAR2 (1);

    lc_conc_segments     VARCHAR2 (500);
BEGIN

  BEGIN

    SELECT chart_of_accounts_id, chart_of_accounts_name
      INTO lc_coa_id, lc_coa_name
      FROM gl_sets_of_books_v gsb, hr_operating_units hou
     WHERE hou.organization_id = p_ou_name
       AND hou.set_of_books_id = gsb.set_of_books_id;

  EXCEPTION

    WHEN NO_DATA_FOUND

    THEN

      fnd_file.put_line

                  (apps.fnd_file.output,

                  ' ------- Error While Checking Char Of
Acct -------'

                  );

  END;


  lc_conc_segments :=

      p_segment1

    || '.'

    || p_segment2

    || '.'

    || p_segment3

    || '.'

    || p_segment4

    || '.'
```

```
            || p_segment5
            || '.'
            || p_segment6
            || '.'
            || p_segment7;
--fnd_file.put_line (apps.fnd_file.output, ' ------- Before Calling
fnd_flex_ext.get_ccid -------'||lc_conc_segments);
        lc_ccid :=
            fnd_flex_ext.get_ccid ('SQLGL',
                                    'GL#',
                                    lc_coa_id,
                                    TO_CHAR (SYSDATE, 'DD-MON-YYYY'),
                                    lc_conc_segments
                                    );
--fnd_file.put_line (apps.fnd_file.output, ' ------- After Calling
fnd_flex_ext.get_ccid -------'||lc_ccid);
        -- fnd_file.put_line (apps.fnd_file.output,
        --                      'The New CCID Details Is ' || ' ' ||
lc_ccid
        --                      );
        RETURN lc_ccid;
    EXCEPTION
        WHEN OTHERS
        THEN
            RETURN NULL;
    END xx_create_ccid;


--Function
    FUNCTION xx_create_faloc_fun (
        p_loc_seg1    VARCHAR2,
        p_loc_seg2    VARCHAR2,
        p_loc_seg3    VARCHAR2
    )
```

```
    RETURN NUMBER
  IS
    l_application_short_name    VARCHAR2 (50);
    l_key_flex_code             VARCHAR2 (4);
    l_structure_number          NUMBER;
    l_validation_date           DATE;
    l_combination_id            NUMBER;
    l_keyval_status             BOOLEAN;
    l_concat_segments           fnd_flex_ext.segmentarray;
  BEGIN
--fnd_global.apps_initialize (1131, 20563, 140, 0, -1);
    l_application_short_name := 'OFA';
    l_key_flex_code := 'LOC#';
    l_structure_number := 101;
    l_validation_date := TO_DATE (SYSDATE, 'DD-MON-YYYY');
    l_concat_segments (1) := p_loc_seg1;
    l_concat_segments (2) := p_loc_seg2;
    l_concat_segments (3) := p_loc_seg3;


    -- fnd_file.put_line (apps.fnd_file.output, ('API Started'));
     --fnd_flex_server1.set_debugging ('6');
    IF fnd_flex_ext.get_combination_id
                    (application_short_name    =>
l_application_short_name,
                    key_flex_code              =>
l_key_flex_code,
                    structure_number           => 101,
                    validation_date            =>
l_validation_date,
                    n_segments                 => 3,
                    segments                   =>
l_concat_segments,
                    combination_id             =>
```

```
l_combination_id
                              )

        THEN
            fnd_file.put_line (apps.fnd_file.output,
                              ('API Combination Created' ||
l_combination_id
                              )
                              );

        /*  ELSE
            fnd_file.put_line (apps.fnd_file.output,
(fnd_message.get));
            fnd_file.put_line (apps.fnd_file.output,
                              ('API Combination Not Created' ||
l_combination_id
                              )
                              );*/

        END IF;


        COMMIT;
        RETURN l_combination_id;
    END xx_create_faloc_fun;
END xxfa_asset_tran_eam_pkg;
/
```

ASSET TRANSFER FROM LOCATION TO LOCATION

There is a requirement from business to transfer the assets from one location to another or from one employee to another in service-based industry. The volume of transfer is high then it is very difficult to transfer one asset to another for the user

Analysis

We have analyzed the standard solution to reach this requirement. In standard oracle, it is transfer either the individual assets or a range of assets, but not the user desired assets.

Solution

Using the asset transfer the system will call API using this API we have built a custom webADI to transfer the desired values. Process as follows user shall run below request set,' FA Transfer Set' to transfer asset form one unit to other.

- Request Set Name: FA Transfer Set

  Request set triggers the following programs

  FA Transfer Loader Program– File Name to be given as parameter.

  FA Transfer Program– Validate & Book Name defaults initially.

  FA Transfer Report – From & to date to be given as parameter

  Assets to be transferred loaded in the template and template is placed in the server. This path is provided in the parameter of the program FA Transfer Loader Program.

  Initially Parameter in the program (FA Transfer Program) Validation Load Flag as **V**.

  Once all three programs completed data can be verified through the FA Transfer Report.

- Individual program shall be run to transfer the validated data.

  Run FA Transfer Program with Flag **P** in parameters

- Run FA Transfer Report

  View output report for details of assets retired.

Template details

Column	Mandatory/ Optional	Format
ASSET_NUMBER	Mandatory	Numeric
ASSET BOOK	Mandatory	Char
TRANSFER DATE	Mandatory	Date

191

UNITS	Mandatory	Numeric
FROM EMPLOYEE NUMBER	Optional	Numeric
TO EMPLOYEE NUMBER	Optional	Numeric
EXPENSE ACCOUNT	Mandatory	Numeric
LOCATION	Mandatory	Varchar
Batch Name	Optional	Char

RETIRE ASSETS

Business maintain many assets in fixed asset module. There is need to retire series of assets periodically. Through standard program, mass retirement is possible for certain range/parameter. But here business is looking for a program through which any number of assets which are not in series to be retired and looking for a program through which they will provide list of assets with certain   necessary fields for full retirement. Template will be filled and uploaded to the server.

Solution

We built a custom program that would help in retiring range of assets as per defined template. Business team identifies the assets and load into pre-defined template. The same template will be shared with IT team to place the same on the server (particular path). Format of the template to be .CSV always. Later IT team shall provide path to business team, which will be used with parameter along with file name.

User running Procedure

User shall run below request set, to retire mass asset.

- Request Set Name: FA Mass Retirement

    Request set triggers the following programs

    FA Mass Retirement Load Program – File Name to be given as parameter along with file name.csv (M)

    FA Mass Retirement Program – Retirement Date to be given as parameter Open FA Period (M)

FA Mass Retire Report – From & to date to be given as parameter (M)

Initially Parameter in the program (FA Mass Retirement Program) Validation Load Flag as V.

Once all three programs completed data can be verified through the FA mass retire report.

- Individual program shall be run to retire validated data.

  Run FA Mass Retirement Program with **Flag P** in parameters

- Run FA Mass Retire Report

  View output report for details of assets retired.

Template Details

Column	Mandatory/ Optional	Format
ASSET_NUMBER	Mandatory	Numeric
MAJOR_CATEGORY	Mandatory	Char
MINOR_CATEGORY	Mandatory	Char
COMMENT	Mandatory	Char
DATE_RETIRED	Mandatory	Date

CUSTOMIZATION OF FA REGISTER REPORT

The main purpose of a fixed asset register is to keep track of the book value of the assets and allow depreciation to be calculated and recorded for both management and taxation purposes unit wise breakup of the fixed asset along with shared expenses between balancing segments or departments.

Uses of this report

- User can view the asset number, asset creation date, asset capitalization date, proceeds of sale of an asset, Bond value, BOE number and BOE date etc. of an asset.
- User can get to know the PTD and YTD depreciation and the accumulated depreciation for every asset.

193

- The assets can be viewed category-wise opening balances.
- This report is the basis for asset reporting as per company Act.

Solution

By customizing, the report based on the standard FA register and adding the new required columns will suffice business requirement and process as follows in order to use FA register report, user would require performing the following steps:

- Log in to the relevant FA responsibility and access the submit request window
- Select the request –FA Asset Register Report
- Select the asset book.
- Select Period
- Optionally select asset number from and to for which report needs to be run.
- Run the report by clicking on 'Submit'.

There are few consideration has to be taken before running this report to get the accurate data and reconciliation purposes.

- Mass addition are prepared and posted
- Each asset capitalized/CIP is assigned to the correct category of assets.
- All the assets that has been capitalized/CIP have also been accounted.

Mandatory Parameters for running this report

Parameter Name	Mandatory/ Optional	Format
Asset Book Type	Mandatory	Char
Period	Mandatory	Period
Asset Number From	Optional	Numeric
Asset Number To	Optional	Numeric

FA ALERTS

Business requirement is to develop an alert for bonded asset value whenever it reaches 90% consumption of bond value of assets. This alert will be scheduled on daily basis. This alert will trigger alert mail to finance team at the time of 90% consumption of bond value to increase bond value in profile option.

Major Features

As this alert is scheduled on daily basis, whenever bond value reaches to 90% it will trigger mail to 'AccountsPayableIndia@XXX.com'. business team will take necessary action. Custom profile has been set up in which the eligible bond value has been set up and this forms the basis for this alert.

ALERT AND PROFILE

Following are the Alert and Profile Option:

Alert: XX_BOND_AMT_ACTION

Profile Option: XX _BOND_AMT_PROF_OPTION

Application: XX Custom Application

User Profile Name: Bond Amount Profile Option Value

RPA IN GENERAL LEDGER

OBJECTIVE

Objective of this chapter is to explain the importance of Oracle General Ledger Module, Why this module is important for the Client's Management/Leadership team and what is the impact of delayed data input/Process delay/Manual work/any bottlenecks. How a company can increase the efficiency of processes by incorporating the Robotic Automation in their company?. Share the experience from actual Doyensys clients.

INTRODUCTION - GENERAL LEDGER

A general ledger is the foundation of a system used by accountants to store and organize financial data used to create the firm's financial statements.

How a General Ledger Works

Transactions are posted to individual sub-ledger accounts, as defined by the company's chart of accounts.

The transactions are then closed out or summarized to the general ledger, and the accountant generates a trial balance, which serves as a report of each ledger account's balance. The trial balance is checked for errors and adjusted by posting additional necessary entries, and then the adjusted trial balance is used to generate the financial statements.

How a General Ledger Functions with Double Entry Accounting

A general ledger is used by businesses that employ the double-entry bookkeeping method, which means that each financial transaction affects at least two sub-ledger accounts and each entry has at least one debit and one credit transaction. Double-entry transactions, called journal entries, are posted in two columns, with debit entries on the left and credit entries on the right, and the total of all debit and credit entries must balance.

The accounting equation, which underlies double-entry accounting, is as follows:

Assets–Liabilities=Stockholders' Equity

The balance sheet follows this format and shows information at a detailed account level. For example, the balance sheet shows several asset accounts, including cash and accounts receivable, in its short-term assets section.

The double-entry accounting method works based on the accounting equation's requirement that transactions posted to the accounts on the left of the equal sign in the formula must equal the total of transactions posted to the account (or accounts) on the right. Even if the equation is presented differently (such as Assets = Liabilities + Stockholders' Equity), the balancing rule always applies.

What Does a General Ledger Tell You

The transaction details contained in the general ledger are compiled and summarized at various levels to produce a trial balance, income statement, balance sheet, statement of cash flows, and many other financial reports. This helps accountants, company management, analysts, investors, and other stakeholders assess the company's performance on an ongoing basis.

When expenses spike in a given period, or a company records other transactions that affect its revenues, net income, or other key financial metrics, the financial statement data often doesn't tell the whole story.

In the case of certain types of accounting errors, it becomes necessary to go back to the general ledger and dig into the detail of each recorded transaction to locate the issue. At times, this can involve reviewing dozens of journal entries, but it is imperative to maintain reliably error-free and credible company financial statements.

The Balance Sheet Transaction Example

If a company receives payment from a client for a $200 invoice, for example, the company accountant increases the cash account with a $200 debit and completes the entry with a credit, or reduction, of $200 to accounts receivable. The posted debit and credit amounts are equal.

In this instance, one asset account (cash) is increased by $200, while another asset account (accounts receivable) is reduced by $200. The net result is that both the increase and the decrease only affect one side of the accounting equation. Thus, the equation remains in balance.

Example of an Income Statement Transaction

The income statement follows its own formula, which can be written as follows:

Revenue−Expenses=Net Income (NI) or Net Profit

It is possible for an accounting transaction to impact both the balance sheet and the income statement simultaneously.

For example, assume that a company bills its client for $500. The accountant would enter this transaction into the accounting ledger by posting a $500 debit (increase) to accounts receivable (a balance sheet asset account) and a $500 credit (increase) to revenue, which is an income statement account. Debits and credits both increase by $500, and the totals stay in balance.

What is Accounting?

Accounting is the process of recording financial transactions pertaining to a business. The accounting process includes summarizing, analyzing, and reporting these transactions to oversight agencies, regulators, and tax collection entities. The financial statements used in accounting are a concise summary of financial transactions over an accounting period, summarizing a company's operations, financial position, and cash flows.

What is a T-Account?

A T-account is an informal term for a set of financial records that uses double-entry bookkeeping. The term describes the appearance of the bookkeeping entries. First, a large letter T is drawn on a page. The title of the account is then entered just above the top horizontal line, while underneath debits are listed on the left and credits are recorded on the right, separated by the vertical line of the letter T.

A T-account is also called a ledger account.

Understanding T-Account

In double-entry bookkeeping, a widespread accounting method, all financial transactions are considered to affect at least two of a company's accounts. One account will get a debit entry, while the second will get a credit entry to record each transaction that occurs.

The credits and debits are recorded in a general ledger, where all account balances must match. The visual appearance of the ledger journal of individual accounts resembles a T-shape, hence why a ledger account is also called a T-account.

A T-account is the graphical representation of a general ledger that records a business' transactions. It consists of the following:

- An account title at the top horizontal line of the T
- A debit side on the left
- A credit side on the right

Example of T-Account

If Barnes & Noble Inc. (BKS) sold $20,000 worth of books, it will debit its cash account $20,000 and credit its books or inventory account $20,000. This double-entry system shows that the company now has $20,000 more in cash and a corresponding $20,000 less in inventory on its books. The T-account will look like this:

T- Account Recording

For different accounts, debits and credits may translate to increases or decreases, but the debit side must always lie to the left of the T outline and the credit entries must be recorded on the right side. The major components of the balance sheet — assets, liabilities and shareholders' equity (SE) — can be reflected in a T-account after any financial transaction occurs.

The debit entry of an asset account translates to an increase to the account, while the right side of the asset T-account represents a decrease to the account. This means that a business that receives cash, for example, will debit the asset account, but will credit the account if it pays out cash.

The liability and shareholders' equity (SE) in a T-account have entries on the left to reflect a decrease to the accounts and any credit signifies an increase to the accounts. A company that issues shares worth $100,000 will have its T-account show an increase in its asset account and a corresponding increase in its equity account:

T-accounts can also be used to record changes to the income statement, where accounts can be set up for revenues (profits) and expenses (losses) of a firm. For the revenue accounts, debit entries decrease the account, while a credit record increases the account. On the other hand, a debit increases an expense account, and a credit decreases it.

T-Account Advantages

T-accounts are commonly used to prepare adjusting entries. The matching principle in accrual accounting states that all expenses must match with revenues generated during the period. The T-account guides accountants on what to enter in a ledger to get an adjusting balance so that revenues equal expenses.

A business owner can also use T-accounts to extract information, such as the nature of a transaction that occurred on a particular day or the balance and movements of each account.

RPA IN GENERAL LEDGER

Some of the automation activities in general ledger modules are discussed below;

DIRECT INTERFACE TO GL

When the organization is dealing with multiple legacy systems, some are interfaced trough sub-ledgers and some are interfaced directly to general ledgers — this type of transaction we see in Cadency business of organization. We see two types of interface in GL.

- User import from journals and upload using WEBADI
- Data push to GL_interface using Custom Program

Analysis

The extract will contain the entire necessary GL Journal data elements required to successfully create Journals in General Ledger. Cleansed Data will be provided as a flat CSV file which will be loaded into custom interface table. Cleansing is not in scope of this conversion program. In case any derivation rules fail the validation step, where ever possible a default value will be used. Required application setups must be completed before running the standard General Ledger Documents Open Interface program.

The scope of the conversion is to load data from the data files to the staging tables, validate the data, load the data into Interface tables and then call Standard GL Import Program to Load data into GL tables. Source System for data load will be AS400 or R11i only and all the other criteria will be as specified in CV40 Document. Posting of Journals need to be performed manually only.

Solution

The solution for this conversion requirement can be broken into two parts, the loading of data into the temporary staging table and the processing and translation of that data before it is passed to interface table to populate standard Oracle base table using the open interface program.

The first step is the data file is loaded into the staging table using the load program. Once data file has been processed, any SQL Loader log files, discard files, and bad files should be concatenated together and copied to the appropriate directory and file where the user may review them. After each run, the load program should accomplish any necessary cleanup.

The second step is the data validation program. This PL/SQL based program should be able to select records from staging table and process those records before processing them using open interface. The incoming data file will be written to a staging table by the load program. The validation program will select these records and process them accordingly. The validation program will have to maintain counts for total records processed, total records with errors, total errors and total records with zero value. The program should also identify any records with errors on the execution report.

Once the data in staging table is validated for all records without errors then valid data is inserted into standard open interface table.

In case any errors then errors needs to be corrected in coma delimited ASCII flat file and again processing needs to be started from first step.

The Third step is Standard Journal Import program will be submitted. This program will process the data from the interface table and insert them into standard GL tables.

DRILL DOWN REPORT

With Oracle R12 Subledger accounting method (SLA) has been introduced which is a rule-based model which helps sub-ledgers to move the information to general ledger. The main use of SLA is to represent multiple accounting process using a single business input which helps business to report both corporate and legal/Fiscal Accounting requirements.

SLA is mainly divided into three parts

1. Journal Import

2. Drill down

3. Data reference from sub-ledger

Analysis: Drilldown functionality enables users to navigate from a Journal in General Ledger to the Subledger Journal Entry in SLA and from there to the transaction which has resulted into that journal.

To get the transaction reference and drilldown we have to go journal line and then drilldown to transaction, it is time-consuming process and hard to identify the differences.

Solution: To achieve this there should be a central report which should provide all the information from GL to SLA to Transaction distribution. Using this report you can get the related information like for AP invoice, PO and receipt data and quantity ordered and received. This report suffices all reconciliation and transaction-related information. Using this we can reconcile major financial areas like Debtors, Assets, Creditors and Accrual.

Data taken from:

https://orafinappssetups.blogspot.com/2013/02/drilldown-in-r12.html

GOODS IN TRANSIT REPORT

Concept of goods in transit/ In transit value report is used to identify the goods transferred from one organization to another. Usual occurrence of this case was when the sender organization sends the goods and received organization is yet to receive goods, actual goods are in transit.

Analysis

Oracle Standard In transit value report is used to Intrasit values, but items that are being transferred between organizations using the in-transit transfer method then only it will appear. They have been issued by the sending organization but not yet received by the receiving organization. For the current organization, this includes transfers out where the Freight On Board (FOB) point is Receipt, and transfers in, where the FOB point is Shipment. But if any company is having intercompany goods transfer then the shipment will happen normally. In this case Intransit value report will not provide the values in the report. So user has to customize to fit the requirement.

Solution

In order to tally both Sender and recipient books, there should be a GIT entry should pass in the recipient books. We have created a report for reconciliation and a Program to collect GIT info and post the GIT journals. A report which will get the data from sender organization and compare with the receiver organization receiving and provide you the in transit value and in parallel one more program will pass information in the GL interface by Debit the GIT account and CR the liability and in the subsequent month it will be reversed by automatic reversal. For reconciliation we can use the report.

AP TDS SLA MODIFICATION

After GST comes in with lot of structural changes, All accounting and ERP software providers come up with the solution with GST to override VAT and service tax. Oracle also comes up with Patch which will add additional Menu's and responsibilities to access GST and made a single folder for both GST and TDS configuration. It made very easy work in single responsibility for both consultants and Users.

Post GST architecture changed for TDS user stated facing issue in accounting. IN old TS-user was able to identify what is the amount for each section after deducting or it can be identified using Supplier site. Each Section is created as each site for Supplier so that System picks up the supplier site whenever you enter the section code in the main invoice. It is very difficult to say what is the value deducted by each section code. It will be needed for some statutory purposes and Reporting from GL.

Analysis

Post GST, We have option to select only one trading partner and site for Income-tax authority. Based on this configuration it is not possible to select the section code wise Supplier sites. We have decided to go with SLA customization based on the section code available in Paygroup of the Income-tax supplier invoice.

Solution

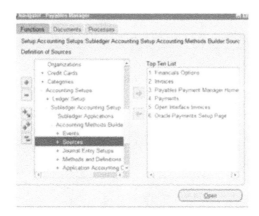

To achieve this solution, we have come up with SLA custom source using a PL/SQL function by passing the invoice ID to the source and the result is the desired value. Desired value was stored in a lookup by providing Meaning as Section code and Description as desired account value.

Navigate to Payables Super user > Setup >Accounting setups> Sub ledger accounting setup >Accounting method and builder > Sources >Custom source.

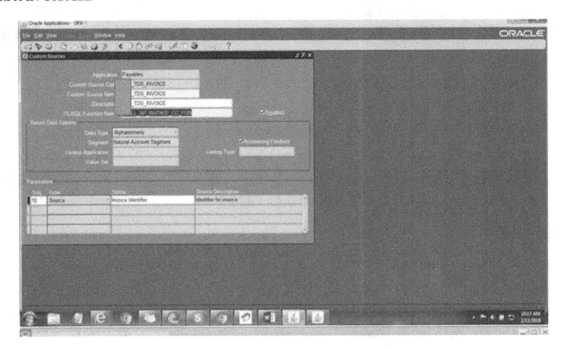

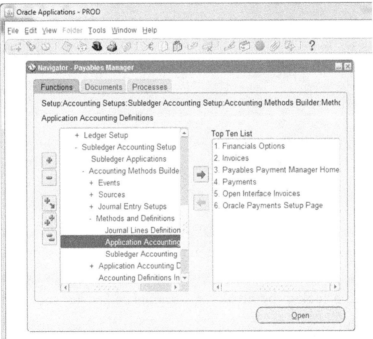

Navigate to Payables Super user > Setup >Accounting setups> Sub ledger accounting setup >Accounting method and builder >Methods and definitions > Application Accounting definitions.

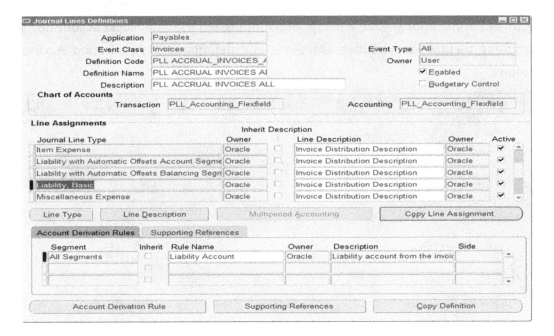

Click on ADR

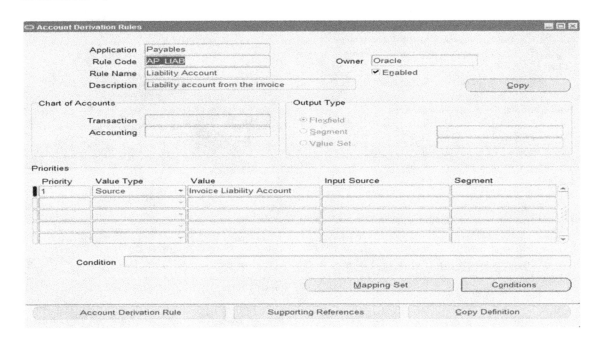

Click on New

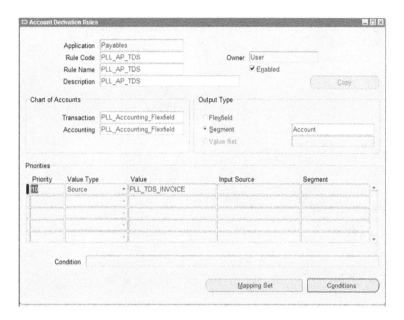

Click on Conditions

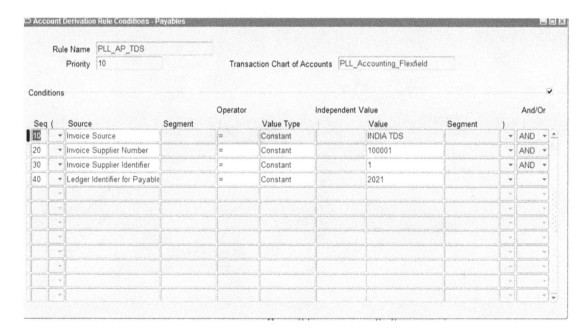

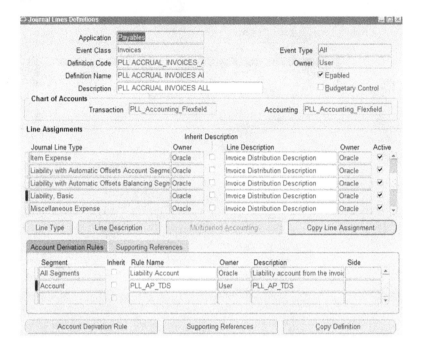

Add the same rule to Credit memo also

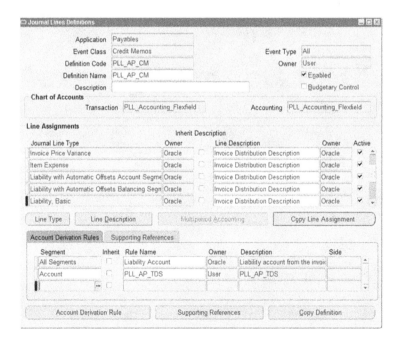

After saving Run the Validate Application Accounting definition Program.

THIRD-PARTY TOOLS FOR RPA

OBJECTIVE

Objective of this chapter is to share Doyensys experience in using other third-party tools, that can help in the Robotic Process Automation.

CONFIGSNAPSHOT

Rookery software team has provided a tool called ConfigSnapShot. This tool is very helpful for any organization who uses Oracle. The major purpose of the tool is to migrate setups across multiple instance or environment using following options

- PlayBack
- API
- WebADI

This tool can effectively migrate the setup data without any many errors and can help in achieving more than 80% timesaving's in setup migrations.

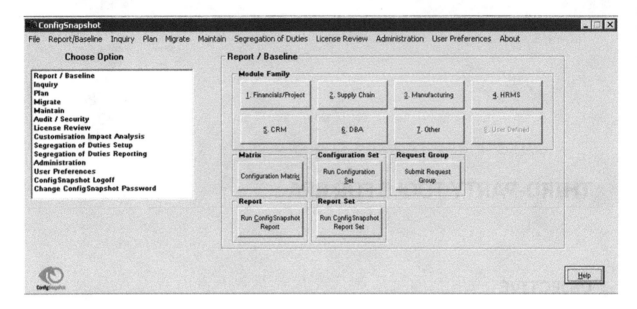

Apart from setup migrations the tool can also be used for the following

- BR100 creation
- Auditing
- SOX Control reports
- Create backup of setups as baselines
- Patch analysis
- Object analysis

Advantages of CSS

- Enormous cost and time saving
- Accurate setup migrations
- Improve system management and administration
- All setup migrations are supported by Oracle as we use Oracle approved migration methods
- Effective audit control
- Compare and analysis of setups or custom objects

Use case

For a global Data Management company, we got an opportunity to use CSS for migration of setup activity and BR100 creation. The client was performing an extension project to implement Oracle to 50 countries. Initially the plan was to use a manual approach to setup all countries. It was estimated to consume approximately 5 to 7 working days with 7 to 10 resources to complete one country.

At the same time it was estimated that by using CSS the migration time can be reduced as much as 70 %. 3 resources can complete the setups migration for 5 counties in around 3 days — this saved enormous cost and time reduction for the client.

BIBLIOGRAPHY

1. Automation – Wikipedia
   https://en.wikipedia.org/wiki/Automation
2. Glossary of civil engineering – Wikipedia
   https://en.wikipedia.org/wiki/Glossary_of_civil_engineering
3. Have you considered the risks and controls before implementing RPA?
   https://www.capgemini.com/no-no/2019/02/have-you-considered-the-risks-and-controls-before-implementing-rpa/
4. Everything you need to know about Robotic Process Automation (RPA)...
   https://www.esspl.com/everything-you-need-to-know-about-robotic-process-automation-rpa-and-rpa-tools/
5. RPA Tools: Which One to Choose? | Future RPA
   https://www.futurerpa.com/post/rpa-tools-which-one-to-choose?lang=hi
6. "What is workflow" Keyword Found Websites Listing | Keyword...
   https://www.keyword-suggest-tool.com/search/what+is+workflow/
7. Business process flows overview | Microsoft Docs
   https://docs.microsoft.com/en-us/dynamics365/customer engagement/customize/
8. How to Get Started Building and Organizing Your Workflow

   https://gravityflow.io/articles/how-to-get-started-building-and-organizing-your-new-workflow/

9. Gerbert, P., Grebe, M. and Hecker, M., et al (2017). *Powering the Service Economy with RPA and AI.* [online] Bcg.com. Available at: https://www.bcg.com/publications/2017/technology-digital-operations-powering-the-service-economy-with-rpa-ai.aspx [Accessed 31 Aug. 2019].
10. Corporation, Oracle. "What Setups Are Needed to Use the Sweep Invalid Distributions in Receivables? (Doc ID 1988458.1)." Support.oracle.com, July 2016, support.oracle.com/epmos/faces/DocumentDisplay?_afrLoop=163978117995895&id=1988458.1&displayIndex=2&_afrWindowMode=0&_adf.ctrl-state=9mxxy305k_121.

11. Gonfalonieri, Alexandre. "How Amazon Alexa Works? Your Guide to Natural Language Processing (AI)." Medium, Towards Data Science, 31 Dec. 2018, towardsdatascience.com/how-amazon-alexa-works-your-guide-to-natural-language-processing-ai-7506004709d3.

ABOUT DOYENSYS

Doyensys, started in December 2006, is a rapidly growing Oracle technology-based solutions company located in the US with offshore delivery centers in India.

We specialize in Oracle e-Business Suite, Oracle Cloud, Oracle APEX Development, Oracle Fusion, Oracle Custom Development, Oracle Database, and Middleware Administration.

We provide business solutions using cutting-edge Oracle technologies to our customers all over the world. Doyensys uses a viable Global Delivery Model in deploying relevant and cost-effective solutions to its clients worldwide. A winning combination of technical excellence, process knowledge, and strong program management capabilities enables Doyensys achieve global competitiveness by making technology relevant to its customers.

We improve business efficiencies through innovative and best-in-class Oracle-based solutions with the help of our highly-equipped technical resources. We are an organization with a difference, which provides innovative solutions in the field of technology with Oracle products. Our clientele across the globe appreciate our laser focus on customer delight, which is our primary success parameter. We have more than 250 resources across the globe. The technical capability of Doyensys stands out from the crowd as we not only provide services of exceptional quality for various Oracle products on time but also take credit for having developed our own products such as DBFullview, EBIZFullview, DBIMPACT, SmartDB, etc.

Our customers are fully satisfied with our services and appreciate our work as we stretch beyond their expectations. We do not compromise on quality for delivery, and the policies of Doyensys revolve around PCITI [Passion, Commitment, Innovation, Teamwork, and Integrity].

Doyensys encourages its employees to participate in Oracle conferences across the globe, and our team has presented papers at various conferences such as AIOUG Sangam, OATUG Collaborate over the years.

The exemplary work of Doyens as a team has created a wonderful environment in the organization. The policies framed by the management are very flexible and employee-friendly, keeping in mind the growth and interest of the organization.

We received 'India's Great Mid-size Workplaces' award (Rank #19) based on the feedback given by our employees in strict confidence and evaluation of various parameters by Great Place to Work. We are an equal opportunity employer and do not discriminate based on sex, religion, gender, nationality, etc. Our women are given a lot of flexibility to work in the organization, understanding the time that they need to spend with their family.

We are also proud to share that we received the award 'Best Workplaces for Women' from Great Place to Work and were ranked among the top 75 in IT and BPM Best Workplaces.

Among the TOP 75 of India's Best Workplaces in IT & IT-BPM 2019

The culture to excel is at the heart of everything Doyens do. We not only share and care for other folks within the organization but also for the folks around the globe.

We have Database and Oracle EBS blogs available on the Doyensys page and are accessible on the internet. These blogs are exemplary work done by Doyens from the knowledge and experience gained by supporting various customers across the globe. There is a habit of creating reusable components for the teams within Doyensys so that a similar piece of work can be helpful for some other project within the organization.

The management is very supportive and encouraging, which is very much visible from the awards [Passion and Commitment, Commitment and Customer Delight, Rookie of the Year] that are given to Doyens, who excel in various categories.

Doyensys is not only a great place to work but is also a great place to learn as employees are always encouraged to explore new technologies and suggest innovative ideas that can benefit the clients. The teams within Doyensys are always encouraged and recognized by the management to add value to the work that is delivered to the customer rather than just doing monotonous work.

ABOUT THE AUTHORS

ANAND RAJENDRAN

 Anand Rajendran started his journey in Oracle as a functional finance consultant in 2005. He has received many appreciations and awards from organisations and clients wherever he worked. He was promoted gradually to different levels, and currently, he is working as "Competency Head – EBS Functional practice" and "Account Manager" at Doyen Sytems Pvt. Ltd. Anand is an experienced Oracle Finance Functional Consultant, having worked in this area for more than 14 years. He is an engineer holding three degrees by choice and ended up in Oracle by passion. Since childhood, he has been very passionate about designing items based on requirement—this paved the way for learning new technologies and achieved success in many projects. With his vast exposure in different phases of project life cycle coupled with his strong skill sets in Order2Cash, Procurment2Pay, requirement gathering, designing, reporting and documentation, he was able to complete every project successfully. His work experience covers implementation, upgradation, developing RICEW components, enhancement and problem management. He possesses strong skills in managing a team and is a great leader. He is also a presenter of Oracle papers at various forums like AIOUG and is very active in blogging

(http://oraclemasterminds.blogspot.com/).

ANIL KUMAR A.B.

Anil has 13+ years of experience in supply chain domain. He has implemented and supported software applications for automobile, healthcare, agriculture, food processing, oil and gas exploration companies in India and abroad. He has grown from a management trainee position to Subject Matter Expert in a span of 13 years. He has completed his Masters from a leading Management Institute from Chennai. He is passionate about writing blogs, travelling and is a foodie.

GOPI KRISHNA

Gopi has 10+ years of experience in the finance domain. He has implemented, supported and upgraded software applications for EPC, healthcare, broadcasting, food processing, oil and gas exploration companies in India and abroad. He has grown from a finance trainee position to Subject Matter Expert in a span of 10+ years. He has completed his Masters from a leading Management Institute from Hyderabad. He was inspired by one of his managers, Varun Gandhi, and started exploring new areas. He is passionate about writing blogs and travelling.

NAGARAJU MUTAKARATAPU

Nagaraju Mutakaratapu is an IT professional with more than 8+ years of experience. He started his career in 2011 as an associate and has been employed in a wide variety of information technology positions, including Business Analyst, System Analyst and Principal Finance Functional Consultant. His core areas of interest include designing solutions and integrations with new technologies. During his career, he has designed and implemented various modules in Oracle financials and has done multiple customisations as a part of the ERP designing.